Handbook
of
Knots
and
Splices

CHARLES E. GIBSON

Handbook
of
Knots
and
Splices

and other work with
hempen and wire ropes

BARNES
&NOBLE
BOOKS
NEW YORK

1996 Barnes & Noble Books

ISBN 1-56619-771-6 *casebound*
ISBN 0-76070-314-0 *paperback*

Printed and bound in the United States of America

MC 9 8 7
MP 9 8 7 6 5 4 3 2

FG

Acknowledgement

I AM indebted to Messrs British Ropes Ltd of London, England, and the Plymouth Cordage Company of Plymouth, Massachusetts, for much of the information in Chapters 1 and 9.

Contents

Foreword

SOME people earn their living by using ropes. They are the
professionals; and whilst I hope that even they may pick
up a wrinkle or two here and there, this book is not directed towards them. It is for the amateur, using that word
in its true meaning of 'unpaid', not 'unskilled'; the man,
woman, boy or girl who needs to use hempen and wire ropes
in order to pursue his or her hobby or recreation; the yachtsman, the climber, the scout, the 'do-it-yourself' enthusiast.

Its aim, first and foremost, therefore, is to be practical
and simple. It takes no knowledge for granted, yet even the
person who already knows something about the subject, will,
I think, learn more, for I have endeavoured to be as compre-
hensive as possible.

But 'all work and no play makes Jack a dull boy' and
there are considerable opportunities for 'play' with ropes
besides skipping. Therefore, not the whole book is strictly
practical; space is spared for some fancy knots and other
forms of decorative ropework, so that after you have completed your work safely by using the correct hitches and
splices, you can settle down to adorn your surroundings
with attractive decoration in fine, clean rope.

To achieve the best possible results in work with rope
you need to know something about its structure and other
qualities. Chapters 1 and 9, therefore, deal neither with
knots nor splices but, respectively, with hempen and wire
ropes as such.

For a similar reason, Chapter 8 deals with various types of blocks and purchases.

This book does not claim to provide a ready-made answer for every problem you are likely to face in using ropes. To do so would be to invite the inevitable, unforeseeable situation for which a solution can only be worked out on the spot; but it does try to explain the principle underlying rope construction and usage, and with these allied to common sense some solution will usually be found.

PART ONE

HEMPEN AND SYNTHETIC ROPES

CHAPTER ONE

The construction and care of ropes

LONG ago men discovered that certain fibres, short in themselves, could be spun into long threads of considerable combined strength and they applied this discovery to the manufacture of cloth and many other articles, including— by no means the least important—rope.

I. ROPE-MAKING MATERIALS

In different times and places since then they have used many materials for rope-making, mainly vegetable in origin until the nineteenth century produced metallic wire rope and the twentieth man-made fibres. Today the materials you are most likely to encounter are:

Vegetable

Hemp. Although once the commonest material for rope-making and the one which gave its name as a general description for fibre ropes, hemp is now hardly used at all commercially. Nevertheless a relatively small amount is still produced for yachtsmen, climbers, etc., and indeed the highest grade of hemp rope is more than one and a half times as strong as the finest manila. Hemp rope lasts well, is easy to handle, does not swell when wet and loses little, if any, strength when lightly tarred. New, it should be a soft golden colour throughout, unadulterated with whitish jute.

13

Jute. This is used principally for cheap strings, clothes lines, etc. It has a distinctive smell.

Manila. This makes a strong, smooth, hard fibre rope much favoured by yachtsmen, which is never tarred as it does not rot when wet, although water makes it swell. Under load, it stretches up to thirty per cent. New, it should be a light buff colour with no fibres sticking out at right angles to the strands.

Sisal. Another hard fibre rope, made from the leaves of East African aloes. Sisal is white, almost as strong as manila and very serviceable. It stands up well to sea water but swells when wet and is liable to be slippery.

Cotton. New cotton rope is white, smooth, soft, smart and pliable, which make it very suitable for fancy work and for running over blocks. However, it is not as strong as manila, and once wet rapidly becomes hard, dirty and weak, although rope of Egyptian cotton remains softer than that of American.

Flax. This is used, sometimes mixed with hemp, for high quality, smaller cords such as smooth strong twines and plaited log-lines, etc. It also makes very strong, durable ropes, but because these are expensive, they are usually made only to order.

Coir. Coir rope (sometimes called **Grass Line**) is made from the husk fibres of coconuts. It is cheap, very rough, very elastic—it stretches up to fifty per cent—and light enough to float on water, but it has only a quarter the strength of manila and far less durability. Moreover, it soon rots if not dried before being stowed away.

Synthetic, man-made fibres

Nylon. Weight for weight, this makes the strongest rope of all, animal, mineral or vegetable, plus which, thanks to its elasticity, it has an ability to withstand sudden shock loading that makes it ideal for climbers. This quality, however, is a disadvantage where a rope must not 'give' at all after having been set up taut, e.g. halyards. Nylon rope has the further attractions of being smooth, completely free from rot or mildew, easy to handle whether wet or dry, resistant to alkaline chemicals and very attractive for fancy work.

Dacron. Although not quite so strong as Nylon, Dacron rope has most of its attractive qualities. It is, however, resistant to acids, not alkalis, and has less elasticity, which, of course, makes it more suitable for certain purposes.

Metallic
Steel. Wires (i.e. long, drawn-out threads) can be made from many metals, but the only one of importance in rope-making is steel. Because steel wire rope differs considerably in structure and handling from hempen and synthetic lines it is treated separately in Part Two.

II. The Structure of Hempen Rope

When reading through a book such as this one, it is best to have a length of rope handy with which to practise the various bends, hitches, knots, splices, seizings and lashings as they are described—on the spot, as it were. If you have such a length by you, examine it now. If you have not, look at figure 1.

The illustration shows a hempen rope of three separate **strands** which have been twisted together so that, as you look at them, they spiral away from left to right. It is, therefore, **a right-handed, hawser-laid rope.** Since the vast majority of ropes in ordinary, everyday use are of the same construction, it is probable that yours, too, is hawser-laid.

However, in your length, the strands, whilst still three in number, may spiral away from right to left, In that event, yours is **left-handed, hawser-laid rope.** It is possible, though, that your rope has four strands, not three, laid up right-

Fig. 1

handed round a central heart. If so, it is **shroud-laid rope.** Or, if it is large, it may be **cable-laid,** formed of three right-handed ropes laid up together left-handed.

Finally, your rope may have more than four strands, either twisted together, which produces a rope smoother than three-stranded but not so strong, or plaited, over and under each other. The latter is **braided rope,** which is smooth, strong and non-kinking.

Opening out a strand of rope (Strand II in Fig. 1) reveals a number of **yarns,** laid up in the opposite direction to the strands to give the rope flexibility (except in certain specialized lines such as non-kinkable rope used for boats' falls).

Teasing out a yarn reveals the **fibres** which have almost invariably a right-handed twist.

In the U.S.A. the size of a rope is commonly given by its diameter, or thickness, although its circumference may also be used. (In Britain, rope sizes are always given as circumferences.) The size of the yarns which make up the rope are based upon the number of a particular thickness of yarn needed to make up *one strand* with a diameter of ½ in. Thus a standard rope of 3 in. circumference will contain three strands each of ½ in. diameter and each strand will contain 18 yarns. The size of these yarns is therefore said to be "18s". Smaller ropes will be made of smaller yarns, which will be known by higher numbers since more of them would be needed to make up a ½-in. diameter strand. The reverse applies to ropes larger than 3 in. circumference.

In Britain, rope sizes are generally varied by using different numbers of standard sized yarns, 24 of which are needed to make a strand of ½ in. diameter.

Ropes for general usage are laid up with a **standard** or **plain lay,** but others may be twisted up exceptionally tight and hard, which gives them a **firm** or **short lay,** or more loosely than normal, which gives them a **soft** or **long lay.** A short laid rope is less liable to lose its shape through absorbing water but will be weaker and less pliable than a standard rope, whilst for a long laid rope the advantages and disadvantages are exactly reversed.

Most ropes are 'oil spun', i.e. treated with a special lubricant during manufacture to soften the fibres. The few which are not are termed 'dry spun'.

Ropes intended for prolonged use in water are 'tanned' or 'barked' or treated with a special waterproof dressing, but those which will be wetted only occasionally, e.g. by rain through being exposed to the weather, are merely soaked in tar. Tarring makes a rope stiffer and heavier and reduces its strength by one-seventh if firm laid, one-sixth if plain laid and one-third if soft laid.

III. The Strength of Ropes

Obviously, even the strongest rope will break if too much is asked of it, so wherever possible, first check that your rope is strong enough to stand up to the work you intend to give it. ('Wherever possible' was inserted into that last sentence because, in an imperfect world, occasions can arise where all that you can do is to grab the best rope to hand, make it fast and hope!)

Especial care is necessary when you are going to hoist or lower heavy objects and for this reason the strength of a rope is always expressed as the strain under which it will break when a load is suspended by it. A rough-and-ready guide to this strength, which errs on the side of safety by producing a figure which is *below* the correct one, is that *new* hemp or manila will break under a load, in tons, equal to the square of its circumference (or size) divided by three. Thus for a 1-in. manila, the breaking strain is

$$\frac{1 \times 1}{3} \text{ tons} = \frac{1}{3} \text{ ton};$$

for a 2-in. manila,

$$\frac{2 \times 2}{3} \text{ tons} = \frac{4}{3} \text{ tons};$$

and so on.

Naturally, consulting a table of **breaking strengths,** such as is given opposite, is preferable to an approximate rule, but such a table is not always readily available. In any case, no rope should ever, knowingly and deliberately, be subjected to a load anywhere near its breaking strength. In fact, only half the latter should be taken as **the safe working load.** Moreover, it is simple common sense to remember that ropes weaken with age, use and exposure to weather.

A Table of Breaking Strengths

Size of Rope		*High*	*Federal Specification T-R-605*		*Nylon*	
Circumference	*Diameter*	*Grade Manila*	*Manila*	*Sisal*	*and Goldline*	*Dacron*
in.	*in.*	*in.*	*in.*	*lbs.*	*lbs.*	*lbs.*
$\frac{5}{8}$	$\frac{3}{16}$	—	450	360	1,100	1,050
1	$\frac{5}{16}$	1,316	1,000	800	2,960	2,650
$1\frac{1}{4}$	$\frac{7}{16}$	1,736	1,750	1,400	5,500	4,800
$1\frac{1}{2}$	$\frac{1}{2}$	2,632	2,650	2,120	7,200	6,100
2	$\frac{5}{8}$	4,984	4,400	3,520	11,000	9,000
$2\frac{1}{2}$	$\frac{13}{16}$	7,896	6,500	5,200	—	—
3	1	11,200	9,000	7,200	26,500	20,000
$3\frac{1}{2}$	$1\frac{1}{8}$	14,900	12,000	9,600	36,000	21,500
4	$1\frac{5}{16}$	19,100	15,000	12,000	47,500	28,000
$4\frac{1}{2}$	$1\frac{1}{2}$	23,800	18,500	14,800	60,000	36,000
5	$1\frac{5}{8}$	29,000	22,500	18,000	74,000	45,000
$5\frac{1}{2}$	$1\frac{3}{4}$	34,700	26,500	21,200	90,000	53,000
6	2	40,900	31,000	24,800	107,000	61,500

Notes: (*a*) The figures for manila and sisal are based on three-stranded, hawser-laid ropes. Four-stranded ropes are approximately 10% lower and nine-stranded cable-laid ropes approximately 33% lower in tensile strength.

(*b*) Numerous intermediate sizes of rope are made, especially amongst the smaller cords. Approximate breaking strengths for these can be obtained by interpolation between the sizes given in the table.

(*c*) There are other standard grades of manila rope between High Grade and Federal Specification T-R-605 minimum.

(*d*) Standard Italian hemp rope is approximately of the same strength as High Grade manila but special, high grade climbers' hemp rope is some 60% stronger.

WEIGHTS OF ROPE
PER 100 FEET

Size of Rope (Circumference)	High Grade Manila	Federal Specification T-R-605 Manila	Nylon & Goldline	Dacron
in.	lb.	lb.	lb	lb.
$\frac{9}{16}$	—	—	0·97	1·5
$\frac{3}{4}$	2*	—	1·74	2·45
1	4	2·84	2·65	3·60
1½	7	7·35	6·95	8·40
2	13	13·1	10.6	12·8
2½	20	19·1	—	—
3	29	26·5	27·5	30·0
3½	39	35·2	35·0	40·0
4	51	46·9	44·0	53·0
4½	64	58·8	55·0	68·0
5	80	73·0	68·0	84·0
5½	97	87·7	84·0	98·0
6	114	105·0	100·0	117.0

*Size $\frac{7}{8}$ in.

Notes: (a) The figures for manila are for three-stranded hawser-laid ropes. Four-stranded shroud-laid ropes are slightly lighter and nine-stranded cable- or water-laid ropes slightly heavier.

(b) Other synthetic ropes are:

Polyethylene: Just over half the weight, two-thirds the strength of Dacron.

Monofilament polypropylene: Slightly lighter and stronger than polyethylene.

Multifilament polypropylene: Slightly weaker than Dacron but only two-thirds the weight.

IV. SMALL STUFFS

'Small stuff' is the sailor's expression for the many smaller non-standard lines. Some of the most common are:

Boltrope. Strictly speaking, not always 'small' as it ranges in size from ½ in. to 6 in. It is a good quality, soft laid pliable rope sewn to the edges of sails to strengthen them.

Hambro' Line. A three-yarn, right-handed tarred soft hemp made in two sizes.

Houseline. Three-yarn tarred hemp, left-handed.

Marline. Two-yarn tarred hemp, left-handed.

Spunyarn. Two, three or four yarns twisted together and soaked in Stockholm tar. Smaller amounts are supplied in balls and larger in coils.

Samson Lines. Very light and similar to fishing lines, they are sold in 30-fathom hanks.

Seaming Twine. A three-ply, high-quality, flaxen twine of which a 1-lb. hank contains some 1,800 yards.

Roping Twine. Similar to seaming twine but five-ply.

Machine Twine. A high-quality, either two- or three-ply twine chemically treated to resist rot and mildew, of which a ball or cop contains about 2,000 yards.

A Nettle is two yarns twisted tightly together to make another, larger yarn and is used for small lashings and hammock clews. **A Fox** is twisted against the natural lay and is used for small seizings.

V. Looking After Your Ropes

1. Kinks in a rope reduce its strength. Therefore always properly coil loose ends, or the whole rope when no longer in use, and hang up the coil or stow it neatly on a shelf, deck or ground. A right-handed rope should be coiled right-handed, i.e. clockwise, and a left-handed rope anti-clockwise.

2. When breaking open a new coil of rope, read the instructions on the label, if any. If there are none, lay the coil so that you can lead off the end you have decided to start with, i.e. either the inside or the outside, *anti-clockwise*. If you lead it off the other way (and all directions

are reversed, of course, for a left-handed rope) it will kink. To remove these kinks, coil it down anti-clockwise, pass the end through the centre, pull it from under the coil and coil down again. Repeat this operation—called **thorough-footing a rope**—two or three times. An alternative, if you have a boat, is to pay the rope out astern whilst under way, tow it for a while to remove the kinks and haul it in, coiling it correctly.

3. Where necessary, dry a rope before stowing it.

4. A rope may shrink or swell when wet. Therefore remember to loosen such things as tent guy ropes if it rains or at night when a heavy dew is expected, otherwise they will become too taut and, at the least, weakened, if not broken.

5. Try to avoid 'nips' in the lead of a rope, i.e. taking it round sharp corners or over sharp edges. If these do not actually cut the inside strands, they may unduly stretch and weaken the strands on the outside of the turn.

6. When using a rope through a block or pulley, make sure that the latter is large enough to take the rope comfortably.

7. Where a rope is liable to be constantly rubbing against something else whilst in use, protect it with chafing gear (see Chapter 7) or worm, parcel and serve it (see below).

8. Periodically twist open a rope's strands to look for signs of rotting in the heart. A rope is rotting if its fibres become soft and brittle or if its heart appears charred. Rust-coloured fibres are a warning sign in manila and hemp and an all-over greyish tinge in coir rope.

9. Where a rope is in constant use over a long period, endeavour to vary the points where it passes through blocks, etc., or these will become weak spots, for, as with

the proverbial chain, the strength of a rope is in its weakest point. If possible, occasionally turn a rope in use end to end, so that all stresses are reversed.

10. The strength of a rope depends ultimately on the friction between fibres. Therefore, if any part becomes frayed or rotten, cut it out and splice the sound parts together again (see Chapter 5).

11. The friction between fibres is increased by their being twisted together. Frayed yarns and unlaid strands are therefore weaknesses, so never allow the end of a rope to become unravelled. Either whip it, back splice it, or point it.

VI. WHIPPING THE END OF A ROPE

Whipping is binding the end of a rope with twine or thread, preferably waxed. Whatever the type of whipping used, the binding must be tight and start away from the end of the rope and work towards it.

To make a Common Whipping. *1.* Lay the non-working end

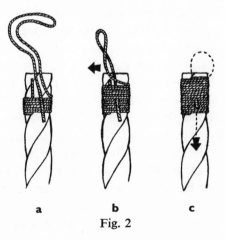

a   b   c

Fig. 2

of the twine along the rope near its end. *2.* With the working end, bind over the non-working end against the lay of the rope, until you are four or five turns off its end. *3.* Lay the working end of twine along the turns you have already put on and hold it in place with your thumb (Fig. 2*a*). *4.* Put on four or five more turns over the working end (Fig. 2*b*). *5.* Pull the working end through tightly and cut off so that no ends of twine are visible, both being hidden and held by the turns (Fig. 2*c*).

An American Whipping is similar to a Common but the non-working end is laid back whilst the last four or five turns are being put on so that they do not cover it. Both ends therefore protrude from the middle of the whipping when completed. Reef knot them and cut off.

In the middle of a rope, a **West Country Whipping** is easier to put on. *1.* Middle the twine on the rope. *2.* Take the ends round opposite ways, half-knotting them each time they meet.

A Sailmaker's Whipping will stand harder wear than other whippings and looks neater. *1.* Unlay the rope for about 2 in. *2.* With the strands pointing upwards, drop a loose loop of twine over one strand, bringing the ends back between the other two and making one end longer than the other (Fig. 3*a*). *3.* Holding the loop and ends with your left hand, re-lay the rope with your right. *4.* Bind the long end of twine against the lay of the rope into a tight whipping of the required length (Fig. 3*b*). *5.* Pass the loop over the *top* of the strands it already encircles and haul on the short end to tighten it. *6.* Pass the short end up the only hollow between the strands which has not already a portion of twine following it and reef knot it to the long end in the middle of the rope (Fig. 3*c*). Cut off.

This whipping on a four-stranded rope requires *two* loops

to start with as in figure 3*d*. Each is later passed over the top of its own strand and loop I is hauled tight first by pulling on loop II.

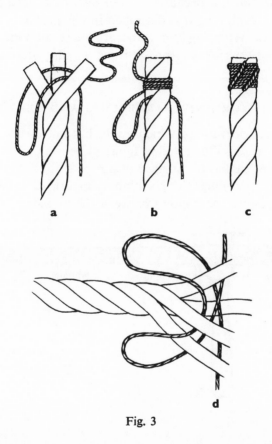

Fig. 3

Snaking on a large plain whipping adds security and decoration. *1*. Pass the twine through the rope with a needle. *2*. Pass the twine round the rope once, back and forth across the whipping, alternately over and under its top and bottom turns. *3.* Pass the twine back through the rope.

Pointing a rope is the most durable, sightly way of protecting its end but because it is considerably more complicated than whipping it is described in Chapter 7.

A Coach Whipping, an elaborate piece of fancy work not usually performed on a rope, is also described in Chapter 7.

VII. Worming, Parcelling and Serving

These three operations, which often, but not invariably, go together, are all illustrated in figure 4.

Worming makes the surface of a rope smooth and round ready for parcelling. Simply bind spunyarn or some other small cord into the hollows between the strands.

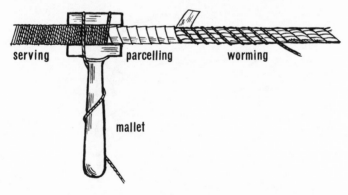

Fig. 4

Parcelling gives a firm surface for serving but has a use in itself in that it prevents water from entering and attacking the rope. For this reason, when parcelling a rope that is, or will be, vertical rather than horizontal, always start from the bottom and work upwards, for parcelling is simply binding strips of cloth, two or three inches wide, preferably of old, tarred canvas, round the rope *with the lay* so that each turn overlaps the edge of its predecessor.

Serving, the final, protecting surface, is spunyarn bound tightly and closely round the rope *against the lay*. It must be put on tightly and is therefore better done with a **serving mallet** (Fig. 4) than by hand; and also more easily by two people than by one, so that one person can pass the ball of spunyarn round whilst the other is actually putting on the turns with the mallet. A serving should be finished off like a Common Whipping.

Remember:

> Worm and parcel with the lay
> But always serve the other way.

CHAPTER TWO

Hitches with a single end

I. THE JAMMING TURN

A HITCH holds because of the friction set up between two surfaces of rope pressed together, which is why hitches with slippery rope or wire are not so efficient. A simple **Round Turn** round a wooden post will resist a considerable pull if the end is held by hand (Fig. 5) as mountaineers know, for

Fig. 5

they use it around their ice axes to belay each other. Hence also the description of someone suddenly stopped from doing something: that 'he was brought up with a round turn'.

More than one turn or, better still, figure-of-eighting round two posts or bollards or around a belaying pin or a cleat, is more efficient, but the resistance of the hold is enormously increased if the last turn is taken as **a jamming turn.** In figure 6 the rope has first been taken for a round turn, then figure-of-eighted round the cleat and finally 'jammed' so that the part of the rope on to which the strain is coming, called **the standing part,** now rides over the part further removed from strain, called **the loose end.** Now, the greater the pull on the rope, the more tightly will the

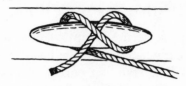

Fig. 6

standing part jam down on the end and prevent it from slipping through.

But, *be warned*! Such a jamming turn should never be taken with any rope that may need to be freed in a hurry, e.g. the sheet of a sail, for it may have jammed so tightly as to defy quick release.

Taking the jamming turn off the cleat in figure 6 reveals simply a loop (Fig. 7), consisting of: I, the loose end (which

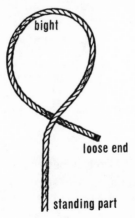

Fig. 7

here, and throughout the book, is shown whipped in order to aid identification); II, a loop or bight; III, the standing part. This loop is the basis of most hitches.

II. Hitches on a Hook

The quickest way to secure a rope's end to a hook is to use a **Blackwall Hitch,** which is just the basic loop made round its neck (Fig. 8). The standing part jams down on the end and holds it more firmly than the illustration might suggest; but if the rope is greasy, a **Midshipman's Hitch** is better. Make a Blackwall and then pull the underneath part forward and place it over the bill of the hook (Fig. 9).

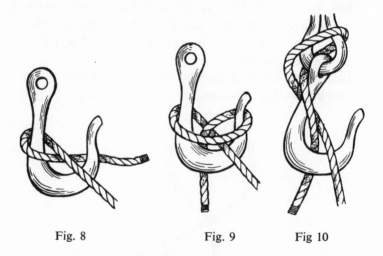

Fig. 8   Fig. 9   Fig 10

A **Double Blackwall Hitch** is better still (Fig. 10). *1.* Place the bight of the rope across the strop to which the hook is attached. *2.* Cross the parts behind the strop and back to cross again in the hook itself, with the standing part being on top of the loose end at both crossings. (In figures 8, 9 and 10 the end has been curtailed for easier illustration. For safety, it should be longer than is shown.)

III. Stopper Knots

Stopper knots are put on to a rope to stop the end from unravelling, to prevent it unreeving through a block or to provide a handgrip. The simplest is the **Overhand Knot** (or **Thumb Knot**). Make the basic loop, pass the end up through the bight and haul taut (Fig. 11).

Fig. 11   Fig. 12

Taking the loose end round the standing part first and passing it down through the bight makes a **Figure-of-Eight Knot** which is easier to undo than an Overhand after being subjected to strain (Fig. 12).

The bulkiness of an Overhand Knot can be increased by passing the end through the bight a number of times before tightening or by making it with the end doubled over.

IV. Securing at a Right Angle

When a rope is made fast for some purpose, the direction from which the strain will come is most commonly at right angles to the point of attachment, whether that be another rope, a wire, post, hook, bollard, rock, ice axe, etc. The simplest 'right-angle' hitch is to take the rope round the securing point and make a **Half Hitch** on its own standing part. (Figure 13 shows that this is nothing more than an Overhand Knot made round something.)

One Half Hitch will probably not hold, but **Two Half Hitches,** with one backing the other, usually will (Fig. 14). However, the standard 'right-angle' hitch is to take a full **Round Turn and Two Half Hitches,** as shown in figure 15, which might have the end stopped back to the standing part for added security, although this is not essential.

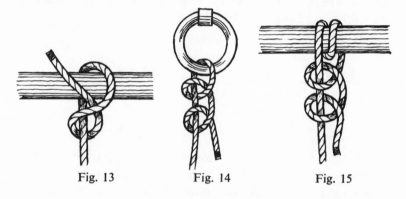

Fig. 13   Fig. 14   Fig. 15

These three hitches, which have not been described in detail as they are better followed from the illustrations, all have the disadvantage that they may jam very tightly if subjected to a heavy strain, especially if the rope is wet. Thus, where the rope is certain to become wet, e.g. in securing to the handle of a bucket that is to be lowered into water, or to the ring of an anchor, the **Fisherman's Bend** is preferable, as it will not jam. *1.* Take a full, but loose, round turn. *2.* Make a Half Hitch by passing the end round the standing part and through the round turn. *3.* Back this with another Half Hitch that does not pass through the round turn and, if desired, stop the end to the standing part (Fig. 16).

A **Clove Hitch** is really two Half Hitches in opposite directions alongside each other. It is easy to make and loosen after strain and particularly useful where the loose

Fig. 16

end has to be kept free to pass on to some other purpose. *1.* Take one round turn on one side of the standing part. *2.* Make a second round turn on the other side. *3.* Tuck the loose end through this second turn and haul taut (Fig. 17). Where the securing position has an open end, a Clove Hitch can be made very quickly either at the end or in the middle of a rope by slipping on two loops as shown in figure 17.

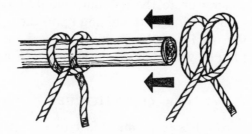

Fig. 17

The Stunsail Halyard Bend is a variation of the Clove Hitch in which the end, instead of being passed through the second round turn, is taken outside it and passed under the first round turn.

Another variation is the **Ossel Hitch** (Fig. 18). *1.* Take one round turn to the left of the standing part. *2.* Take a second to its right but in the opposite direction. *3.* Pass the end outside the second turn and through the first one.

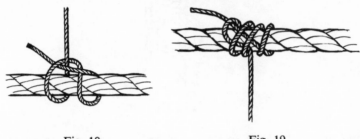

Fig. 18   Fig. 19

This hitch takes its name from the ossels which are the short lengths of rope with which fishermen join the backing of their nets to the headrope. On the backing they use an **Ossel Knot,** a very reliable hitch. *1.* Place your left thumb on the rope and take a round turn over it and the rope, coming up to the left of the standing part. *2.* Take a second turn also coming up to the left but missing your thumb. *3.* Take two more turns both coming up to the right of the standing part. *4.* Finish by passing the end through the small bight left by your thumb and haul taut (Fig. 19).

V. 'PARALLEL' HITCHES

Sometimes a rope has to be made fast to an object that lies roughly parallel to the direction of strain, e.g. in suspending something from a vertical pole or the shrouds of a yacht. The best general purpose hitch here is a **Rolling Hitch** (Fig. 20). Make this like a Clove Hitch but take *two* round turns

Fig. 20

on that side of the standing part from which the strain will come before crossing the end over to make the final jamming half hitch. Always put a Rolling Hitch on a rope *against the lay*.

A **Stopper Hitch** is a variation of the Rolling Hitch, useful for securing the tail of a handy billy to a rope as shown in figure 21 or in putting a temporary stopper on a rope in order to take the strain off its loose end whilst this is being

Fig. 21

moved to a new securing position or taken to a winch. Start like a Rolling Hitch but instead of putting on the final half hitch, dog the loose end round the rope *with the lay* and stop it.

A Timber Hitch, used for securing a plank or spar that has to be hoisted or towed, is a Half Hitch taken with a rather long loose end which is then dogged back round itself *with the lay* (Fig. 22). Haul on the standing part to

Fig. 22

tighten the hitch. To keep the end of the timber pointing in one direction, slip on another Half Hitch as shown in figure 22.

VI. LOOPS IN A ROPE

A Bowline makes a loop, large or small, in the end of a rope which has a thousand and one uses. *1.* Place the loose end from right to left across the standing part leaving a loop of the required size. *2.* Grip the end and standing part together with the right hand—tips of the fingers are best—and twist downwards to the left, i.e. clockwise, for half a turn. This will bring the end poking up through a small loop (Fig. 23*a*). (You can, of course, make this loop first and poke the end up through it, but the other way is vastly quicker.) *3.* Pass the end behind the standing part and down through the loop again (sometimes described as 'putting the rabbit back in his hole'.) *4.* Haul taut (Fig. 23*b*).

A Running Bowline produces a noose, or sliding loop, which should never be used to hoist a person as his own

weight would tighten the rope unbearably around him. *1.*
Pass the end right round the standing part and lay it across
its own part as shown in figure 24. *2.* Continue as for a
simple bowline.

a   b
Fig. 23

To lower or hoist a person, two loops are needed, one to
go under his armpits and the other under his thighs. One
way to provide these is to make a **French Bowline** (Fig. 25).

Fig. 24   Fig. 25

1. Start as for a simple bowline, stages 1 and 2. *2.* Instead of passing the end behind the standing part, take it right round in front of it to make another large loop. *3.* Pass the end up through the small loop again, round the standing part and back through 'the Hole' as for a simple bowline.

An alternative, which has the advantage that it can be made in the middle of a rope thus leaving two long ends free for hauling, is the **Bowline on the Bight.** *1.* Make a bight in the rope and using both parts together follow stages 1 and 2 of a simple bowline (Fig. 26*a*). *2.* Holding the loop firmly, bring the bight projecting through it down towards you and up behind the knot to the position shown in figure 26*b*. *3.* Haul taut with both parts together and work the loops to the different sizes needed to fit under the armpits and the thighs.

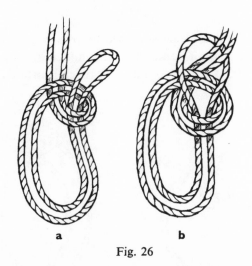

a   b

Fig. 26

The Man Harness Hitch is another way of making a loop in a rope without using the ends. *1.* Make a loop of the required size as in figure 27. *2.* Pass the bight 'A' up between 'B' and 'C'. *3.* Bring 'D' and 'E' together and haul taut with 'A'.

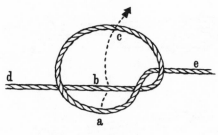

Fig. 27

VII. Miscellaneous Hitches

A Sheepshank is used to shorten a rope temporarily or to 'by-pass' a weak point in it. *1.* Gather in the amount desired, including the weak section if there is one, as in figure 28*a*. *2.* With the standing parts slip a Half Hitch over either end of the loop as in figure 28*b*. *3.* For added security, either toggle or seize the bights left protruding to the standing parts. (Figure 28*c* shows, at the left-hand end, a toggle, at the right-hand a seizing.

A Catspaw makes a temporary loop in a rope for hooking on. *1.* Throw back a bight as in figure 29*a*. *2.* Twist the two loops away from each other. *3.* Bring the two small eyes thus formed together and insert the hook (Fig. 29*b*).

A Marline Hitch lashes up long bundles, e.g. hammocks, or bends a sail to a spar as shown in figure 30. *1.* Make an eye in the end of the rope (a small bowline will do). *2.* Pass the other end round the bundle, through the eye and haul taut. *3.* Continue along the bundle with a series of Half

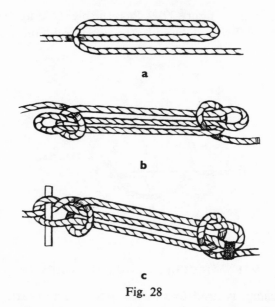

a

b

c

Fig. 28

Hitches which should be in line, hauling each taut as it is made. *4.* Finish with a Clove Hitch instead of a Half Hitch. (See also Fig. 69.)

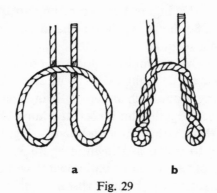

a   b

Fig. 29

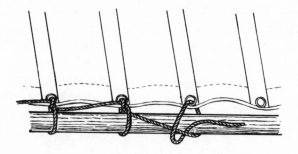

Fig. 30

A Marline Spike Hitch (Fig. 31) is used to obtain a better purchase, or grip, on a small cord. *1*. Make a loop over the standing part. *2*. Pass a spike, bolt or screwdriver, etc., across the loop but under the standing part. *3*. Pull on both ends of the spike to tighten.

Many hitches can be fashioned for quick release by taking the last turn with a bight of rope instead of the end. A Clove Hitch, Rolling Hitch, etc., can be so made. How-

Fig. 31

ever, as many of us know from experience with shoe laces. there is some danger that a bowed hitch may slip, but one that will not—there are others— is a **Draw Hitch.** *1,* Take one bight of rope up behind the bar and another in front of it (Fig. 32*a*). *2.* Pass the front bight through the back one and pull taut with the loose end, which leaves the front bight still standing (Fig. 32*b*). *3.* Make a third bight with the loose end and pass it through bight II. *4.* Pull taut with the standing part (Fig. 32*c*).

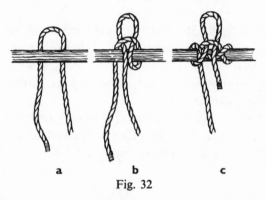

a   b   c

Fig. 32

If a line has to be thrown any distance it needs a weight on the end in order to make it carry. If this line will be frequently so used, e.g. a boat's heaving line, this weight can be a big, heavy knot called **A Monkey's Fist.** *1.* Make a hank of three or four turns near the end of the rope. *2.* Pass the loose end round the waist of this hank three times. *3.* Pass the end through the loops formed at the ends of the hank and round the turns already taken three times (Fig. 33*a*). *4.* Complete stages 2 and 3 twice more. *5.* Work the knot tight. *6.* Either (a) cut off the end close to the knot (Fig. 33*b*) or (b) splice it into the standing part.

A quickly made hitch that will also free easily after being

Fig. 33

under strain, is the **Roadmender's Knot,** which is very suitable for securing a rope along a line of posts but can also be used to make the end fast to just one, e.g. in securing a mooring line to a bollard. *1.* Take a turn round the post with a long bight of rope passing below both the standing part and the loose end (Fig. 34*a*). *2.* Pass the bight over the top of the post and haul taut (Fig. 34*b*).

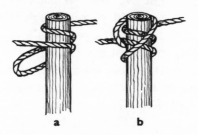

Fig. 34

Mousing a hook is a sensible precaution to prevent the load from jumping out and should be used wherever possible. Simply middle a length of twine on the shank of the hook and take the ends opposite ways round shank and bill a number of times and finish by reef-knotting them. This closes the jaw of the hook.

CHAPTER THREE

Knots joining two ropes

THE knot most commonly used for joining two ropes of similar size is the **Reef Knot,** which everybody knows how to make—or do they? The ropes—or, for that matter, the shoe laces, for we should reef knot these every day—are brought together and half knotted, i.e. twisted one over the other. Then the ends are brought back and again half knotted, and the result, unless you have been careful, is an insecure Granny Knot!

To make a Reef Knot correctly, if, in the first half knot, you took the right-hand end over the [lefthand, coming back you should take the lefthand over the righthand; and *vice versa*. Remember: 'Right over left, left over right' or 'Left over right, right over left'. When completed the two parts of each rope should pass through the bight of the other rope *side by side*. If one part is above, and the other below, the bight, your knot is a Granny.

To free a Reef Knot hold both parts of one rope in one hand and those of the other in the other hand and push together. A Reef Knot is very secure under strain, but because it frees so easily, there is a danger that it may loosen of itself if the ropes are relaxed.

Where the ropes may not be subjected to a continuous pull, a safer hitch is the **Sheet Bend,** which will also join two ropes of unequal size or one rope to the eye in the end of another or to the cringle in the corner of a sail. To make it: *1.* Form a bight in the larger rope (or use the eye if there is one). *2.* Pass the smaller rope up through this bight. *3.* With the smaller rope's end, take a complete turn round

44

both parts of the larger rope and pass it under its own part (Fig. 35). For extra security, especially if the ropes are wet or if one is considerably larger than the other, repeat Stage 3 to make a **Double Sheet Bend.**

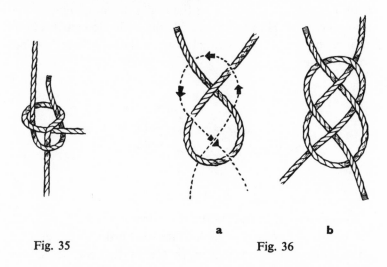

a   b

Fig. 35   Fig. 36

Sometimes what is really a Sheet Bend is used to secure a rope to a hard eye in the end of another rope, but it is taken with the bight, instead of with the end of the rope, for quick release even under strain. Like this it is called a **Slippery Bend.**

A **Carrick Bend** provides another way of joining two ropes of unequal size, especially if they are large. *1.* Form the basic loop (Fig. 7) with the larger rope. *2.* Pass the end of the smaller rope under this loop (Fig. 36a). *3.* Take this end as shown in figure 36a: *over* the larger rope's standing part, *under* its loose end, *over* one side of its bight, *under* the smaller rope's own part, and *over* the other side of the bight. When tightened, the ends come out on opposite sides of the knot and should be stopped to the standing parts if the ropes are large.

One advantage of the Carrick Bend is that it forms a flat knot that does not impede the progress of the ropes round a capstan or winch. If the ropes are not to be so led, however, **Two Half Hitches with the ends stopped back,** as shown in figure 37, are quicker to make; or **Two Bowlines** may be used.

Fig. 37

Where the other ends of the two ropes are already secured, the ends to be joined to each other may not overlap enough to provide slack for making loops, etc. In this case, the **Shroud Knot** described in the next chapter may prove useful.

The quickest way of joining two thin lines is to make an Overhand Knot with both ends together, side by side, but a **Double Overhand Knot** is sounder. *1.* Make an Overhand Knot on the end of one line. *2.* Pass the other line through this knot and make an Overhand Knot with it round the standing part of the first line (Fig. 38).

Fig. 38

Both these knots may prove difficult to undo but loosely twisted lines such as spunyarn or marline may be joined by a **Spunyarn Knot,** which will free more easily. *1.* Split the lines into two and crutch them as in figure 39. *2.* Take strand I over and right round the standing parts. *3.* Take strand III under and right round the standing parts. *4.* Half knot I and III where they meet on top of the crutch.

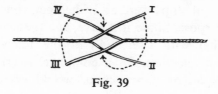

Fig. 39

CHAPTER FOUR

Knots with a rope's own strands

NOWADAYS most knots of this character must be classed as 'fancy', although when the rigging and even the massive anchor cables of ships were all of hempen rope, many had a practical purpose. Some still have, and these are described below, together with a selection of the 'fancy' variety. It can only be a selection, for a complete description of all known examples of 'fancy knots' would occupy a whole volume, far more space than can be spared in a book the prime aim of which is to be utilitarian. However, if you become enthusiastic about 'fancy knots'—decorative work well done in clean, new rope is extremely attractive—the knots below will teach you the basic principles from which you can explore the subject further and even invent your own original examples.

Two simple knots, the Crown and the Wall, form the foundation of most of the more complicated work, as well as being useful in themselves.

A Crown Knot binds together the strands at a rope's end and is the first step towards a Back Splice (see next chapter). To form one: *1.* Unlay the rope. *2.* Bend strand I into a bight towards the centre of the rope. *3.* Bend strand II into a similar bight with its end passing through the bight of strand I (Fig. 40). *4.* Pass strand III through the bight of strand II and work all taut. This knot can also be made by passing each strand down through the bight of its neighbour to the left instead of to the right. Either way the strands, come out at the bottom of the knot.

Fig. 40

In a **Wall Knot**, however, the strands come out at the top of the knot. *1.* Unlay the rope. *2.* Pass strand I outside strand II but inside strand III (Fig. 41*a*). *3.* Pass II outside III and the end of I (Fig. 41*b*). *4.* Dip III outside the bight of II and bring it up through the bight of I (Fig. 41*c*). *5.* Work all taut, cut off the ends and whip (Fig. 41*d*).

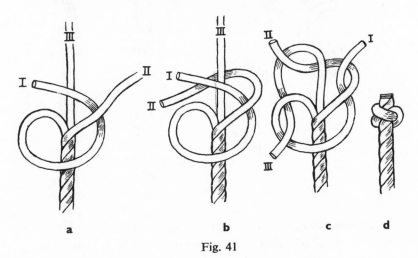

a   b   c   d

Fig. 41

A Wall Knot differs from a Crown in that each strand passes outside its neighbour first before going *upwards* through his bight. Like the Crown, it can also be made to the left.

Both knots can be doubled in size by 'following round'. This means tucking each strand through the knot again following alongside, but not on top of, its original lead and a pricker or marline-spike may be found handy here for loosening the tucks without untying the knot.

A Manrope Knot is a smart, effective stopper at the end of, say, a gangway rope threaded through a row of stanchions. To make it: *1.* Form a Wall Knot. *2.* Form a Crown Knot on top of the Wall (Fig. 42*a*). *3.* Follow round the Wall. *4.* Follow round the Crown (Fig. 42*b*). *5.* Cut the ends close off.

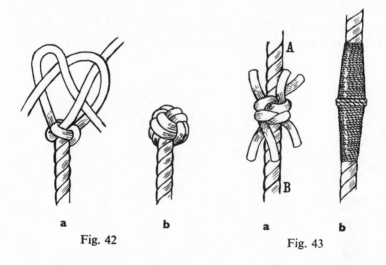

a   b   a   b
Fig. 42   Fig. 43

A Shroud Knot, which, as previously mentioned joins two ropes, is so called because it was used to repair shrouds that had been shot away in action. It makes a join as secure and neat as a splice but requires less rope for its manufacture and is more quickly made. *1.* Unlay both ropes and crutch the strands, i.e. so that each strand passes between two strands of the other rope but in the opposite direction to them. *2.* With the strands of rope 'A' form a Wall Knot round rope 'B' to the left on a right-handed rope and *vice versa* on a left-handed. *3.* Similarly form a Wall with

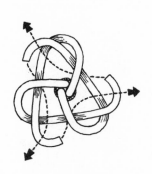

Fig. 44   Fig. 45

the strands of 'B' on 'A'. *4.* Tighten until the knots jam against each other (Fig. 43*a*). *5.* To make a neat finish, marl and serve as in figure 43*b*.

To make a **Stopper Knot.** *1.* Form a Wall Knot but do not work taut. *2.* Pass each end from left to right up through the loop next to it and under the end already there. *3.* Work taut. *4.* Lay up the strands hard, whip and cut off to the whipping (Fig. 44).

The Matthew Walker Knots are also variations on the Wall. To make a **Single Matthew Walker:** *1.* Start like a Wall but pass strand I under both II and III. *2.* Pass II under III and I and come up through the bight of I. *3*. Pass III round the end of I, through its bight and through the bight of II (Fig. 45). This knot differs from the Wall in that each strand passes through the bights of both the others.

In a **Double Matthew Walker,** which completed looks like figure 46*a* and is a knot that will not slip or capsize, each strand passes through *three* bights, i.e. including its own, as shown in figure 46*b*.

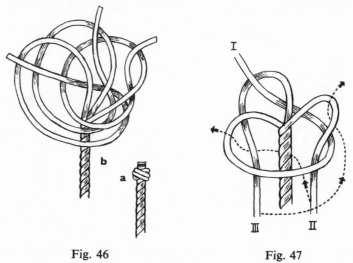

Fig. 46   Fig. 47

A **Diamond Knot** is often made in the middle of a rope. To form one: *1*. Unlay the rope to the point where you wish to make the knot, taking care to preserve the lay as much as possible as you will have to re-lay the rope later. *2*. Lay each strand alongside the standing part so that you leave three bights standing above the point where they fork. *3*. Take strand I outside strand II and up through the bight of strand III. *4*. Take II outside III and up through the bight of I. *5*. Take III outside the bight of I and up through the bight of II to make figure 47. *6.* Re-lay the rope. If each strand is followed round once, this forms a **Double Diamond Knot.**

The descriptions of knots so far have all assumed that you are using three-stranded rope, but the Wall, Crown, Matthew Walkers and Diamond can all be made equally well with four- or six-stranded rope if you apply the basic principle of each particular knot, e.g. that in a Wall Knot each strand passes upwards through the bight of its neighbour; that in a Diamond Knot the strands must first be laid back along the standing part, etc.

A Chequer Knot cannot be made on three-stranded rope as it requires an even number of strands. This, however, makes it very suitable for braided ropes and it is often used on the end of bell lanyards, etc. To form one: *1.* Unlay the strands to a reasonable length (you will need more stuff for this knot than for those described above) and in their centre at the fork place a core of some material (a ball of spun-yarn will do). *2.* Make a Crown Knot left-handed over the core with the even numbered strands. *3.* Make a Crown Knot right-handed with the odd-numbered strands in such a way that they interlace with the even strands (Fig. 48*a*). *4.* With all strands make a Wall Knot right-handed (Fig. 48*b*). *5.* Follow round the Crown Knots and the Wall. *6.* Make a Wall Knot round the bottom of the knot (Fig. 48*c*). *7.* Make a Crown Knot similarly (Fig. 48*d*). *8.* Follow round these last two knots. This forms a Turk's Head. *9.* Finish by tucking each strand away under a strand of the rope just above the whipping, and cut off.

The **Turk's Head** just mentioned is, without doubt, the favourite design in decorative ropework. To fashion one *on the end of a rope* make a Manrope Knot and follow the ends round a second time or more often.

A Turk's Head also forms a decorative knot on the noose of *a knife or whistle lanyard*. Unlay the end of the lanyard and with the strands form a Wall Knot round the standing part of the lanyard itself. Then form a Crown Knot also

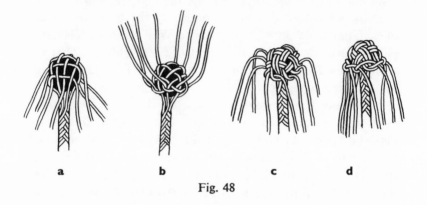

a   b   c   d

Fig. 48

round the lanyard and follow round at least twice. This knot will slide up and down the standing part.

To make *a standing Turk's Head on a lanyard* that will not slide, and therefore forms a loop, not a noose, make the Wall and Crown and follow round as above, but before doing so tuck one strand *through* the standing part.

A Footrope Knot is similar in appearance to a Turk's Head. In the days of sailing ships, it was worked on to the footrope on which the men stood whilst handling canvas aloft, and whilst today that need has almost disappeared, it still makes a decorative handgrip that will not slip because it, too, is worked *through* the rope. To fashion the knot: *1.* Pass two pieces of line through the rope at the same point but tucking each under a different strand. *2.* With the four ends work a Diamond Knot (Fig. 49). *3.* Follow round once or twice and cut off. (More than two pieces of line can be used if desired.)

Fig. 49

A Long Footrope Knot (Fig. 50). *1.* Start as for a Footrope Knot but with longer lines. *2.* Make a Footrope Knot but do not cut off the ends. *3.* Turn the rope end to end and make another Footrope Knot. *4.* Follow round twice and cut off.

Fig. 50

CHAPTER FIVE

Splicing hempen ropes

I. General Remarks

SPLICING is a method of joining one rope to another, or two parts of the same rope, by tucking the strands of one under and over those of the other. When strain comes on to the splice, the strands bite inwards and hold each other in position but it is still safer to assume that a splice reduces the strength of a rope by about one-eighth.

All splices start by unlaying the rope(s) for a certain distance and to begin with it may be found that a temporary whipping at the fork, i.e. at the point where the unlaying ends, may make work easier by preventing the strands from untwisting farther. With practice, however, this whipping may no longer be necessary, especially on smaller ropes. Whipping the end of each individual strand will also help in producing a neater finish to the splice.

All tucks should be made *with the lay of the rope* into which they are being made, unless otherwise directed, and roughly at right angles to its strands. They should be pulled tight along the lay and can be made to lie snugly, which is essential for strength, by stretching and twisting the splice, by rolling it on a table with the palm of the hand or on the floor with the foot, and by hammering the strands home lightly with a wooden mallet.

A completed splice will look neater and gain in strength if it is wormed, parcelled and served.

II. Eye Splices

An Eye, so called from its shape, is a loop, usually at the end of a rope but sometimes in the middle. It may be *hard*, if made around a metal stiffener called a thimble, or soft without a thimble. The most common type of thimble is known from its shape as a **Heart Thimble** (Fig. 51). A **Lanyard Thimble** is very similar but has a flattened top in order to provide a larger opening for turns of rope (Fig. 52). A **Sail Thimble** (Fig. 53) is circular so that it will fit snugly into the canvas.

Fig. 51   Fig. 52   Fig 53

To make an Eye Splice round a thimble. *1.* Unlay the rope for a distance equal to three times its circumference. *2.* Bend the still laid-up end round the thimble to make an eye with the fork of the strands just reaching the standing part, and with the middle and left-hand unlaid strands on top of it (Fig. 54*a*). *3.* Lightly stop the thimble to the crown of the eye. *4.* Tuck the middle unlaid strand from right to left under the strand on which it rests (Fig. 54*b*). *5.* Tuck the left-hand unlaid strand from right to left over the strand under which the first tuck was made and under the next one (Fig. 54*c*). *6.* Turn the rope over to the left so that the right-hand unlaid strand is now on top of it. *7.* Tuck this strand from right to left under the only strand under which a tuck has not already been made (Fig. 54*d*). This completes the first set of tucks. *8.* Tuck each unlaid strand again, over one strand and under one.

To finish off the splice either (a) divide the yarns of each strand into two and whip together each pair of adjacent halves from neighbouring strands (three pairs all told) or (b) scrape or cut off lengthwise half of each strand and tuck again, and then halve and tuck once more. These 'half-tucks' taper the splice to a neat finish which may be served if desired.

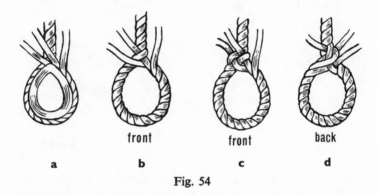

front   front   back

a   b   c   d

Fig. 54

To make a simple Soft Eye. Proceed as above but omit the thimble.

To make an Eye Splice with Four-Stranded Rope. Proceed as above for three-stranded rope but in stage 5 the left-hand strand is tucked under *the same strand* as the middle one (or rather the left-hand one of the middle pair) but comes out from under the strand beyond it, i.e. it passes under *two* strands. The tucking of four separate strands is, of course, necessary to complete the first set.

To make an Eye Splice Wormed and Collared. This is a simple eye Splice with a fancy finish. Carry out stages 1 to 7 of a simple Eye Splice and then — 8. Separate four yarns from each strand (making twelve all told in a three-stranded rope and sixteen in a four-stranded). 9. Keeping these out of the way, with the remainder of the strands carry out stage 8 plus one extra 'half-tuck'. *10.* Lay up the separated yarns into two-yarn nettles. *11.* With one nettle from each yarn, worm to the end of the splice and finish by tucking each nettle under a different strand (Fig. 55*a*). *12.* With the two sets of nettles, those left at the top and those protruding from under a strand at the bottom, fashion Footrope Knots (Fig. 55*b*).

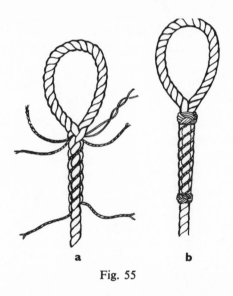

a   b

Fig. 55

To make a Sailmaker's Eye Splice. Proceed as for a simple Eye Splice but *make the tucks from left to right,* i.e. against the lay. This produces a splice neater in appearance but with less strength, which should not, therefore, be used where considerable strain will come upon it.

To make a Single Tuck Eye Splice and Wall Knot. Proceed as for a simple Eye Splice but instead of putting in a second set of tucks after the first, form a Double Wall Knot with the strands round the rope. This splice is useful where the eye at the end of a rope has to run right up to a block or pulley because it takes up less space and cannot jam in the sheave.

To make an Eye in the middle of a rope. Under some circumstances an eye projecting from the side of a rope may be needed. At the point where it has to be made, grip the rope with both hands and twist in opposite directions. This will force out the strands doubled as in figure 56. Continue twisting until they are long enough to be tucked at least twice and with them make a simple Eye Splice.

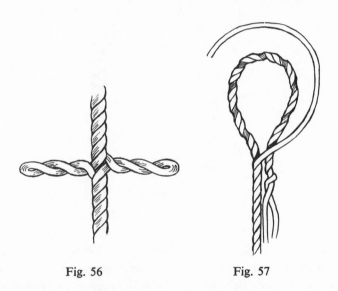

Fig. 56   Fig. 57

To make a Flemish Eye. *1.* Unlay strand I to a distance equal to one and a half times the circumference of the desired *eye*. *2.* With strands II and III form the eye as in figure 57. *3.* Lay strand I back into the space from which it came but in the reverse direction until it returns to the fork. *4.* Unlay strands II and III and, with strand I, scrape them to taper, lay them along the standing part and marl or serve them down to it. This makes a neater-looking but weaker job than an ordinary eye splice. It is, however, useful in the end of a large rope to provide a means of hauling it about.

When making this eye with four-stranded rope, carry out stages 1 to 3. Then unlay another strand, but not one adjacent to that already unlaid, and deal with it as for that strand. Then complete with stage 4.

To make an Artificial or Spindle Eye. Splicing braided ropes is a difficult task because of the tightness of the braiding. To join two braided ropes it is first necessary to unbraid them for a sufficient distance, put on a whipping at this point and then rebraid them as described under 'Round Sennit' in Chapter 7, ensuring that the braiding is looser than it was originally. They can then be short spliced in a way similar to that described below for laid ropes but allowing for the difference in the number and arrangement of strands. However, it must be reiterated that this would be a difficult task for any but an expert.

Making an eye at the end of a braided rope is somewhat easier for, as with a Flemish Eye, no tucking is involved; hence the name: 'Artificial Eye.' Simply unlay the strands for a sufficient distance, form them into an eye and marl them down to the standing part.

A much neater, stronger job, however, is achieved by using a spindle; hence the other name: 'Spindle Eye.' *1.* Take a cylindrical piece of wood or metal—the spindle—the diameter being slightly larger than that of the desired eye and on it raise two lumps with spunyarn about the diameter of the rope apart and half its diameter high (Fig. 58*a*).

2. Lay four pieces of seaming twine along the spindle and stop them in place as shown in figure 58a. 3. Unlay the rope, open the strands and separate each yarn. 4. Hitch the yarns in pairs, one from either side, over the spindle between the lumps—which prevent them from spreading out—until all have been used, varying the positions of the hitches so that they do not all come together, which would raise a bump on the eye (Fig. 58b). 5. Lay the ends of the yarns

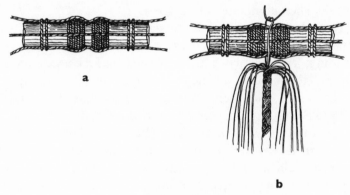

Fig. 58

along the standing part and lightly stop them to it. 6. Cut the stoppers holding the seaming twine and bring its ends together to knot them in pairs tightly over the hitched yarns. 7. Take off one spunyarn lump and slide the eye off the spindle. 8. Starting at the top, serve the eye down to the fork. 9. Take off the stoppers on the ends of the yarns and scrape the latter down to taper. 10. Serve them down to the standing part. 11. (Not essential, but to give a better finish) Cover the eye with cockscombing (see Chapter 7).

III. Joining Two Ropes

Short Splicing. A Short Splice is the easiest way of splicing two ropes together but it is bulky and not suitable on a rope that has to pass through a block or any narrow opening. To make it: *1.* Unlay both ropes to a distance equal to twice their circumference. *2.* Crutch the strands together so that each lies between two strands of the opposing rope (Fig. 59*a*). *3.* Put a stop round the fork. *4.* Tuck each strand of rope 'A' over the strand of rope 'B' immediately to its left (looking towards the end of the strand) and under the strand beyond, as in eye splicing. *5.* Tuck the strands of rope 'A' again, over and under. *6.* Cut off the stop on the fork and tuck the strands of rope 'B' twice into those of rope 'A'. (Figure 59*b*, to make the operation easier to follow, shows only one set of tucks on each rope.) *7.* Stretch the splice by pulling and twisting. *8.* Either (a) whip the ends and cut off or (b) take a few of the underneath yarns from each strand to fill up the lay of the rope by worming, scrape

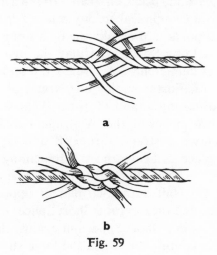

a

b

Fig. 59

the remainder of the ends, marl them down on to the rope with thin twine and serve over the splice.

Two four-stranded ropes are spliced exactly as two three-stranded, but if a three-stranded rope has to be spliced to a four-stranded: *1.* Unlay the three-stranded rope for twice the distance of the four-stranded, split one of its strands into two parts and relay it as a four-stranded rope for the distance needed to take the tucks of the other rope. *2.* Crutch the strands and proceed as above.

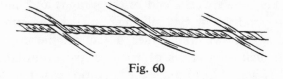

Fig. 60

Long Splicing. Because a Long Splice does not produce a bump, it is used where a rope has to reeve through a block or pulley. However, it uses up considerably more rope than a short splice and occasions can arise when, in fact, it might be more economical to buy a new rope than to cut out the weak portion of an old one by a Long Splice.

To make a Long Splice: *1.* Unlay the two ropes to ten times their circumference. *2.* Crutch the strands as for a Short Splice. *3.* Further unlay one strand of rope 'A' and lay up the opposing strand of rope 'B' in its place until only some two inches of the 'B' strand remain unused. *4.* Similarly unlay one strand of rope 'B' and lay up a strand of 'A' in its place. *5.* Leave the two remaining strands, one of each rope, as they are (Fig. 60). *6.* Finish off in one of these ways: (a) Half knot each pair of opposing strands, taper the ends and tuck as for a Short Splice; or (*b*) tuck the tapered ends as in a Short Splice but against the lay so that each end goes continually round the same strand; or (c) as for (b) but before tucking the ends, halve each one and tuck each half round a different strand to that encircled by its 'twin'. This gives a very smooth finish.

These three methods by no means exhaust the possible endings to a Long Splice. Indeed, it used to be said that 'every ship has her own way of making a Long Splice', and 'Different ships, different long splices!' is still a current expression to indicate that everybody has his or her own way of doing a thing. With practice, you may be able to devise your own personal way of finishing off to produce the perfect Long Splice; one whose very existence is only noticeable in a rope after the very closest examination.

To long splice four-stranded ropes, proceed as for three-stranded but ensure that the four points where strands of the opposing ropes meet are evenly spaced. Do not have two close together.

To long splice a three-stranded rope into one of four strands: *1*. Unlay both ropes and crutch the strands. (You are bound to have a *pair* of the 'four' strands passing between two of the 'three' strands.) *2*. Further unlay one strand of the three-stranded rope and lay in one of the 'four' strands. *3*. Further unlay one of the 'four' strands and lay in one of the 'three', choosing your strands so that the two of the 'four' strands which are left are the pair which were crutched together. *4*. Divide the remaining strand of the three-stranded rope into two unequal portions, a third and two-thirds. *5*. Half knot the one-third portion with one of the remaining 'four' strands. *6*. Further unlay the last 'four' strand and lay up the two-thirds strand in its place. *7*. Half knot all ends and finish as for a simple Long Splice.

If you are in desperate need of a sound Long Splice in cable-laid rope, it might be as well to entrust this task to an expert. On the other hand, if you want to assess your own

ability, try to make a **Mariner's Splice,** for if you succeed
you will have passed one of the old tests of skill! *1.* Unlay
the ends of the cables to six times their circumference. *2.*
Unlay each of the ropes of which the cables are composed.
3. Crutch the strands of each rope with those of the corresponding rope in the other cable in such a way that the three
forks do not come opposite to each other. *4.* Long splice
each pair of ropes into each other as described above.

A Cut Splice. This splice is sometimes used instead of a
Short Splice to join two ropes, as it is easier to make,
although it leaves an even larger lump in the rope. It has a
use in its own right in that it provides an oblong loop in the
middle of the rope. To make this loop: *1.* Cut the rope where
the loop is required. *2.* Splice end 'A' into end 'B' at
position I, tucking as for an Eye Splice. *3.* Splice end 'B'
into end 'A' at position II, tucking as for an Eye Splice
and making sure that you have put your splices where
they will leave a loop of rope between them and not merely
two parts of rope lying snugly side by side. Figure 61 shows

Fig. 61

the right hand splice made and served and the left hand just
commenced.

IV. OTHER SPLICES

Chain Splice. If a length of rope has to be secured to the
end of a chain, it is very likely that the end link will prove
too small to allow the whole rope to be passed through and

brought back to form an eye. In this event it is necessary to make a Chain Splice: *1*. Unlay the rope for about six times its circumference. *2*. Further unlay strand I for a distance equal to the circumference of the eye required plus one more turn. *3*. Pass strands II and III through the end link of the chain and bring them back to form an eye with their still laid-up parts. *4*. Lay strand II into the space left by strand I. *5*. Further unlay strand I for about a foot and lay strand II up in its place. *6*. Half knot strands I and II. *7*. Tuck away the ends of I and II as for a Long Splice. *8*. Tuck strand III as for a simple Eye Splice. Figure 62 shows I and II knotted and the first tuck of III.

Fig. 62

A Back Splice. This is often called 'a lazy man's whipping' because, whilst serving the same purpose of preventing a rope's end from unravelling, it is easier to make than a proper whipping. On the other hand, it is less sightly and thickens the rope, thus making it difficult to reeve through a block. To back splice: *1*. Unlay the rope for three times its own circumference. *2*. With the strands form a Crown Knot. *3*. Tuck the strands back along the rope as for a Short Splice (Fig. 63).

To work a Cringle into a Rope or Sail. A Cringle is a small becket or loop (see Fig. 64*a*). *1*. Take a strand of rope three and a half times the length of becket required. *2*. Tuck one end, tapered, three times into the main rope. *3*. Tuck the other end through the rope so as to leave a loop

of the size required. *4.* Dog this working end back round
the loop, keeping the turns in the natural 'lay' of the
strand. *5.* Pass the working end through the main rope
where the first tuck of the standing end was made. *6.* Dog
the working end back to the other end of the becket, filling
up all the spaces left in the lay (so that, in effect, you have

Fig. 63

laid up a short section of three-stranded rope but using
only one strand). *7.* Finish off by tucking the working end,
tapered, three times into the main rope. (Figure 64*a* shows
only one tuck made.)

To work a cringle on to the boltrope of a sail, proceed as
above, but pass the ends through the eyelet holes in the sail
instead of the rope and finish by tucking them round the
cringle itself (as in figure 64*b*) until they cross under its
crown, where they should be cut off short.

To splice hempen rope into wire. It may sometimes be
necessary to splice the end of a hempen rope into a wire one.
In this event, proceed as for a Short Splice in hempen rope,
working the wire rope in three pairs of adjacent strands.
Make at least six tucks on either side of the crutching point

and marl, parcel and serve over the whole splice when it is complete.

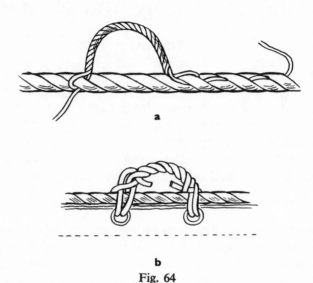

a

b

Fig. 64

If the hempen rope is four-stranded, proceed as described above for splicing three- and four-stranded ropes, treating the wire rope, which has six strands, as being the three-stranded rope, and work its strands, four in pairs, and two singly.

CHAPTER SIX

Slinging, lashing and seizing

I. Slinging

Sling is a general term for any rope designed to be taken round objects to be hoisted in order to hook them to the lifting gear. A **Bale Sling** is a large continuous loop made by short splicing the ends of a rope, although reef knotting them would serve temporarily.

A **Butt Sling** is a single length of rope, one end of which is whipped or pointed and the other eye spliced. A temporary arrangement here would be to make an eye with a small bowline.

To sling a cask, barrel, drum or other cylindrical object (a) **using a Bale sling:** *1.* Place the cask on its side (bung up if it has one and contains liquid). *2.* Pass the sling underneath both ends. *3.* Bring the bights up over the cask and pass one through the other, making sure that they cross in line with the bung. *4.* Hook into the bight that has passed through its partner. (A visit to a newspaper office might provide a fine demonstration of this method, for the men who unload the massive rolls of newsprint are skilled users of a Bale Sling.) (Fig. 65.) (b) **using a Butt Sling:** *1.* Place the cask on its side, bung up. *2.* Reeve the whipped end of the rope through the eye and place the loop thus formed over one end of the cask and haul well taut. *3.* Take the whipped end of the rope round the other end of the cask and clove hitch it to its own part, in line with both the eye and the bung. *5.* Hook on halfway between the hitch and the eye (Fig. 66).

If a cylindrical object has to be slung in an upright position, e.g. a laden drum or cask without a lid, use a single piece of strong rope. *1.* Lay the rope down and stand the cask, head up, fairly centred on its middle. *2.* Bring the

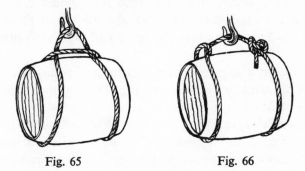

Fig. 65   Fig. 66

rope's ends up and half knot them on top of the cask. *3.* Open this knot out sideways and place the bights thus formed one on either side of the cask. *4.* Reef knot the ends to make a loop for the hook (Fig. 67).

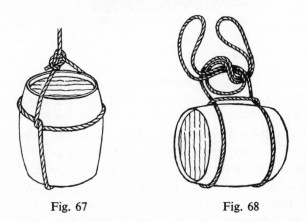

Fig. 67   Fig. 68

To shorten a sling either (a) throw back a bight to make it the required length and twist the two small bights thus formed into a catspaw (Fig. 29) or (b) proceed as described above for hoisting with a Bale Sling but before hooking into the top bight, divide this into two smaller bights and half, or even reef, knot them. (Figure 68 shows them half-knotted.) Then hook into the two small bights left protruding.

A Strop is a smaller continuous loop of rope than a sling and is not usually used for slinging. The two most common strops of hempen rope are:

1. **The Selvagee Strop.** To make this continuous loop of rope *yarns*: *1.* Drive two bolts or large nails into a plank at a distance apart equal to the length of strop required. *2.* Secure one end of a ball of rope yarns to one nail. *3.* Pass turns about the nails with the yarns until the strop is the desired thickness, taking care to pull each turn taut as it is

Fig. 69

made. *4.* Bind the yarns together with a marline hitch, using two-rope yarn on a smaller strop and larger spunyarn on a big one (Fig. 69).

This produces a very pliable strop useful for securing the hooks of tackles, etc. at points where no other suitable attachment presents itself, e.g. on poles, masts, shrouds, tightly set up wires, etc. Wrap it round as in figure 70. On a thick mast, just one turn will be sufficient.

2. **The Grommet.** This is a small, firm, continuous loop better known to the passengers on ocean liners as a deck

quoit. Because its size does not offer enough room for a short splice, it is made from a single strand of rope. To make it: *1.* Unlay a strand of rope three and a half times the circumference of the grommet required, endeavouring to

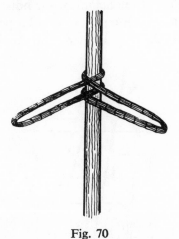

Fig. 70

preserve the natural turns of the lay in the strand. *2.* Close up the middle of the strand into a ring of the desired size (Fig. 71*a*). *3.* Pass the ends round in their original lay until

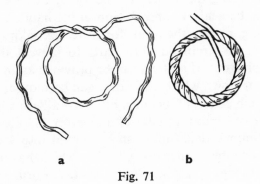

a   b

Fig. 71

all spaces have been filled (Fig. 71*b*). *4.* Finish off as for a Long Splice.

Where a cylindrical object has to be hoisted or lowered and no crane or tackle is available, a **Parbuckle** may prove useful, provided that the height of the hoist is not too great (Fig. 72). *1.* Middle a long rope round a post or pin at the top of the hoist. *2.* Take the two ends under the drum or

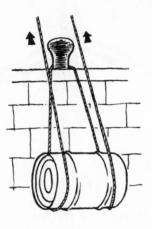

Fig. 72

barrel and bring them back to the top of the hoist, where they are to be held by hand. *3.* Now either haul on the ends for hoisting, or pay them out for lowering, taking care to keep an equal strain on both parts to prevent the drum from slipping out. If a plank can be provided as an inclined plane up or down which the drum can be moved, this will make the job easier. (Truckmen often use a Parbuckle when lowering casks into the cellar of a tavern.)

A continuous Bale Sling can be turned into a carrying sling for an object such as a bottle, which has a rim or flange at its top, by using a **Bottle Knot.** *1.* Form a loop on the sling as in figure 73*a*. *2*. Take bight I under II and bight III over IV (Fig. 73*b*). This produces a centre loop to slip over the neck of the bottle and two side loops as carrying handles.

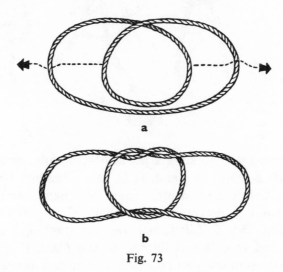

a

b

Fig. 73

The **Bag or Beggarman's Knot** serves the same purpose but more securely and is made with a single length of rope. *1*. Make two loops in the middle of the rope as in figure 74*a*. *2*. Partially cross the right-hand loop in front of the left-hand (Fig. 74*b*). *3*. Pull the left-hand loop half through the right-hand to make figure 74*c*. *4*. Holding the ends I and II firmly with one hand, pass the other hand down through the space 'A' to grip 'B' and pull it through, at the same time allowing the loop 'C' to drop down the back of the knot (Fig. 74*d*). *5*. Haul taut, at the same time working open the centre space which will go over the bottle, and knot or splice the loose ends to make a second carrying loop.

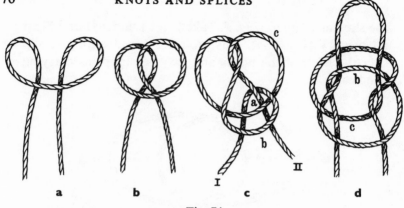

Fig. 74

The safest way to sling a plank horizontally, as a stage on which a man can stand, is to use a **Scaffold Hitch** at either end. *1*. Take two turns round the plank, the second being nearer to its end. *2*. Lay the standing part between them (Fig. 75a). *3*. Lift turn I over the standing part and turn II and loop it over the end of the plank (Fig. 75b). *4*. Bring the standing part and loose end up and secure with a bowline (Fig. 75c).

A Bosun's Chair (Fig. 76a) is a cradle in which a man can sit whilst working down a vertical, or near vertical, object such as a mast, a stay, etc. The seat is a piece of 1-inch planking about 18-in. by 6 in. and the bridle is a strop rove through the hole at each corner of the seat before being spliced. In use, the chair should be held by a lowering line (always called a gantline aboard ship) passing through a pulley or block above, or at the top of, the object on which work is to be performed. The lower end of the gantline may be secured on the ground or deck, or to the chair itself. In the former event, a second person is needed to lower the chair when the man in it wishes to descend even for a short distance; but if the gantline is secured on the chair, he can lower himself by using a **Lowering Hitch.**

1. Secure the gantline to the chair by means of a Double Sheet Bend with the end stopped securely to the bridle. (This is essential, whoever is going to do the lowering.) The hitch can be seen in figure 76*a*. *2.* When hoisted high enough, pass a wracking round both parts of the gantline to take the weight whilst the Lowering Hitch is being made (Fig. 76*a*). *3.* Pull a long bight of the hauling part of the gantline through the strop, pass it over your head and drop it behind

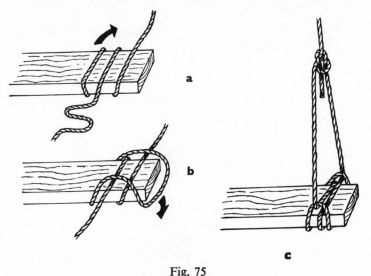

Fig. 75

your feet (Fig. 76*b*). *4.* Pass your feet behind the bight and bring the latter up in front of you (Fig. 76*c*). *5.* Haul taut on the gantline and you will find that you have reef-knotted it to the chair, which it will hold securely.

To lower yourself: cast off the wracking, pull up some slack on the hauling part and allow the gantline to render

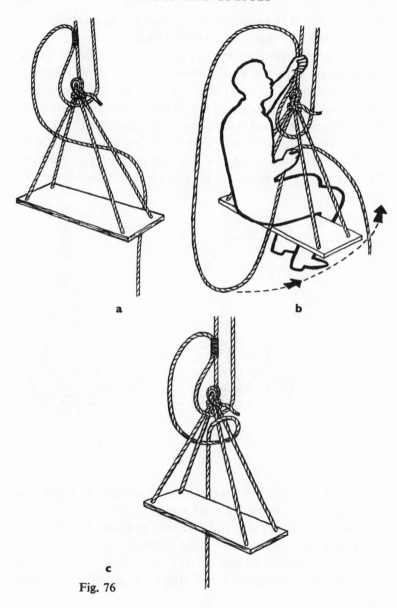

a

b

c

Fig. 76

round, which it will do under your own weight. By keeping the hauling part firmly in hand, you will have the whole operation under control. Nevertheless, it will be as well to practise this hitch first at a very low level, just in case you make a mistake! Similarly, although experienced sailors dispense with the preliminary wracking and merely hold the two parts of the gantline together by hand whilst making the hitch, do not attempt to emulate them until you, too, are experienced. Lastly, remember that in the naval services a man working aloft or over the side must have permission of the officer of the deck and must have a man standing by as a safety factor.

II. LASHINGS

Two spars, e.g. tent poles, masts, scaffolding, sheer legs, trestles, etc. may be fixed together very firmly by a strong rope lashing, the particular type used depending upon the job the spars have to perform. Use:

1. *A Square Lashing* where the spars under load have a tendency to slide over each other, at the corners in figure 77.

2. *A Diagonal Lashing* for bracings where the spars may spring away from each other under load, the centre in figure 77.

3. *A Sheer Lashing* for sheer legs where the spars have to share a load (Fig. 80) or for joining two spars end to end (Fig. 81).

To put on a Square Lashing. *1.* Place the spars in position. *2.* Secure one end of the lashing by a clove hitch to the spar nearest to the vertical. Make the hitch below the point where the other spar crosses, and dog the loose end round the standing part (Fig. 78*a*). *3.* Take turns under and over the 'horizontal' spar, behind the 'vertical' spar and over

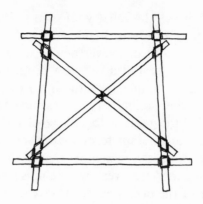

Fig. 77

and under the 'horizontal' as in figure 78b making some
three or four turns and hauling each taut as made. 4. Put
on three or four frapping turns *between* the spars as in figure

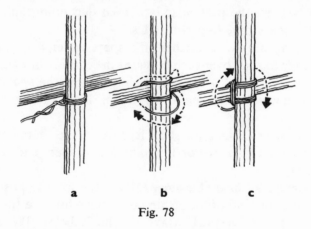

a   b   c

Fig. 78

78c, pulling each very taut and, if need be, beating them
into position. These turns ensure that those of stage 2 will

hold the spars tightly together. *5.* Finish with a clove hitch on the 'horizontal' spar.

To put on a Diagonal Lashing. This should not be put on until the ends of the spars concerned have been securely fixed.

1. Put a tight Timber Hitch diagonally over the crossing (Fig. 79*a*). *2.* Continue with three or four tight turns in the same direction as the hitch and the same number at right angles to it (Fig. 79*b*). *3.* Put on frapping turns between the spars. *4.* Finish with a Clove Hitch over one spar (Fig. 79*c*).

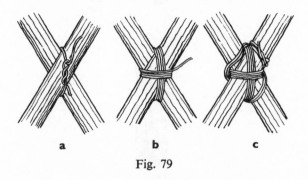

Fig. 79

To put on a Sheer Lashing. *1.* Start with the legs parallel to each other. *2.* Put a clove hitch round one spar and dog the loose end round the standing part. *3.* Take a number of turns around both spars together (ten will generally be enough) hauling each taut as made (Fig. 80*a*). *4.* Splay out the legs to the required angle without allowing the tension on the lashing to ease and put on three or four frapping turns (Fig. 80*b*). *5.* Finish with a Clove Hitch on one spar.

When lashing two poles end to end, carry out stages 1 to 3 as above but begin and end with a Clove Hitch round *both* poles and double the number of turns taken. As there will

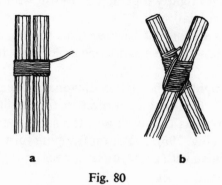

a   b

Fig. 80

Fig. 81

be no room for frapping turns, drive in wedges of wood to tighten the lashing (Fig. 81).

III. Seizings

Seizing is a method of binding two ropes, or two parts of the same rope, together by means of strong, small cord where a splice is not practicable for some reason or other, e.g. because there is not enough room. To be effective, the cord must be bound on very tightly so that if, because of its smallness, difficulty is experienced in obtaining a sufficiently firm grip upon it, use a Marline-Spike Hitch.

The first step in any seizing is to bring the two ropes as close as possible together. This is sometimes difficult to achieve by hand, because they may be already tautly stretched, in which case rig a **Spanish Windlass** as follows:

1. Lay a bar horizontally across in front of the ropes. *2.* With the middle of a length of strong twine take a full turn round the ropes. *3.* Dog each end of the twine back round its own part to form a small eye and with these dogged ends take turns round the bar. *4.* Insert a marline-spike in each 'dogged' eye and lever them round the bar until the ropes are tightly together (Fig. 82). It will be found that greasing

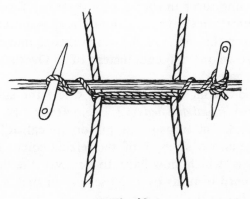

Fig. 82

the middle of the twine allows it to slide more easily round the ropes and bar.

The type of seizing to use depends upon the nature of the strain upon the ropes.

A **Flat Seizing** should be used only where the strain upon both ropes is *equal and light*. *1*. Make a small eye or loop in the end of the seizing cord. *2*. Take a turn with the end of the cord round both ropes, pass it through its own eye and heave taut. *3*. Take as many more turns as are required (at least seven) round both ropes, heaving each taut as made. *4*. Pass the end of the cord down *inside* the turns *between* the ropes and bring it up through the eye at the other end of the seizing (Fig. 83). *5*. Take one complete frapping turn

Fig. 83

round the seizing lengthwise between the ropes. *6*. Take two more frapping turns in such a way that they form a Clove Hitch. *7*. Work an Overhand Knot tight up against the Clove Hitch to stop the end from drawing through and cut off (or make a Crown or Wall Knot instead of an Overhand as they will look neater).

A **Round Seizing** should be used where the strain upon both ropes is *equal and heavy*. *1*. Begin as for a Flat Seizing, stages 1 to 4. The turns so far put on are called 'the lower turns'. The added strength of the seizing comes from 'the riding turns' which now have to go over the 'lowers'. *2*. Take the cord in turns over the seizing in such a way that each turn lies in the hollow between two of the lower turns.

The riding turns are bound to be one less in number than the lowers. *3.* Tuck the end of the cord under the last of the lower turns and haul taut (Fig. 84*a*). *4.* Finish as for a Flat Seizing with the frapping turn and Clove Hitch (Fig. 84*b*).

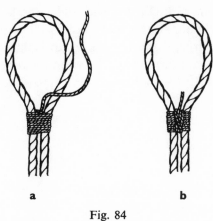

a   b

Fig. 84

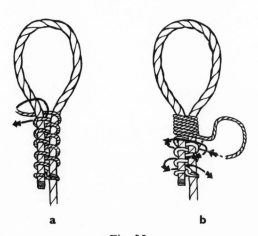

a   b

Fig. 85

A Racking Seizing should be used where the strain upon the two ropes is *unequal*. *1*. Start as for a Flat Seizing with a turn round both ropes and reeve the end through the eye. *2*. Instead of continuing with round turns, dip the end between the ropes and then figure-of-eight it round them a dozen or so times. *3*. Dip the end under the last turn taken (Fig. 85a) and haul all the turns taut. *4*. Now put on tight, round riding turns, working back towards the eye, and after the last one, again dip the end between the ropes (Fig. 85b). *5*. Finish off as for a Flat Seizing.

CHAPTER SEVEN

More fancy work, mats and plaits

I. MATS

ALMOST all rope work—hitching, splicing, fancy work, etc.
—is a development of the basic principle of weaving,
namely the interlocking of strands by passing over and
under each other. The simplest design of rope mat, the **Sword
Mat,** is made on a loom. Within reason, it can be of any
length or width and is not usually intended to be decorative.
Aboard ship it serves for such purposes as the gripes which
hold lifeboats firmly in position on their davits and as
chafing gear laid between a rope or wire and some hard
object against which it is rubbing. It has similar uses ashore.

To make Sword Matting (Fig. 86): *1.* Make a primitive
loom by fixing two bars or tightly stretched ropes parallel

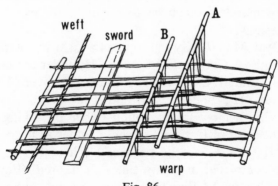

Fig. 86

to each other at a distance apart equal to the length of
matting required, and around them wind the rope which

will form the *warp*. 2. Lay two pieces of wood across the warp and connect 'A' to every odd-numbered strand and 'B' to every even-numbered. 3. Lift up 'A'. This also lifts every alternate strand. 4. In the space between these and the strands not lifted, pass a second rope, called the *weft* across. 5. Drop 'A' and lift 'B'. This also lifts the other set of alternate strands. 6. Pass the weft back in the space between the two sets of strands. 7. Continue in this fashion until you reach the other end of the warp. Each time the weft is passed it must be pressed home firmly with the 'sword', a flat, narrow piece of wood, usually slightly bevelled on one edge. Once the technique has been mastered, sword matting can be quickly made.

A Thrum Mat is also non-decorative, being simply a piece of canvas into which thrums, short lengths of yarn, have been thrust by the bight so that both ends protrude on the same side.

A rope mat for the deck or floor, however, will not only be functionally hard-wearing; properly made in clean, new hemp or manila, it can be a delight to the eye. Here are three designs:

An Oval Mat. *1.* Lay the rope as shown in figure 87*a* in three loops. *2.* Carry end I over end II, under the bight 'A', over 'B', under 'C', over 'D', under 'E', over 'F', under 'G', over 'H', under itself and over 'A'. This forms figure 87*b*. *3.* Now follow round either by taking I back along the path of II, passing over or under as it does, or by taking II back along the path of I. The following round may be completed as many times as desired. (Figure 87*c* shows only once.) *4.* Finish by leaving the ends under strands where they will not be seen.

A Square Mat. *1.* Make the loops as shown in figure 88*a* in the middle of the rope. *2.* Pass the bight 'A' over 'B' and under 'C', but do *not* pass bight 'D' on the other side of the same loop. *3.* Make a loop on end I and pass it under end II (Fig. 88*b*). *4.* Pass the bight 'E' (but not the bight 'F') over 'D', under 'B', over 'C' and under 'A'. *5.* Form

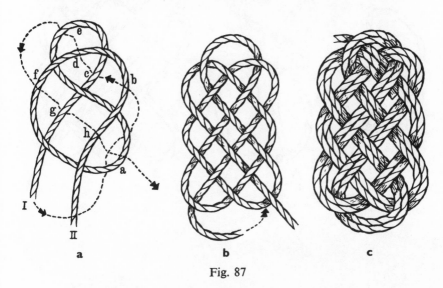

Fig. 87

a similar loop on end II (which will now be to the left of I), pass it under I and similarly pass its uppermost bight only through the design alternately over and under crossing strands. *6.* Repeat this operation of passing a loop under one end, and a bight up through the design, using the two ends alternately, until the mat has reached the desired size. *7.* Finish by passing an end, which has not been doubled into a loop, to the right under the other end and up through the middle of the design, over and under, until it emerges at the top (Fig. 88*c*).

A Carrick Mat. *1.* Make two loops as in figure 89*a*. *2.* Pass end I over end II, under 'A' over 'B', under 'C' and

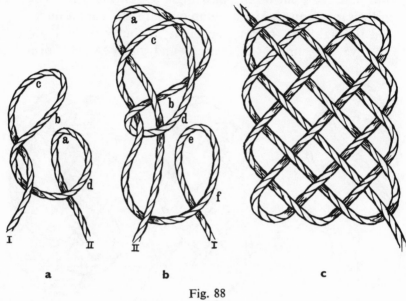

a   b   c

Fig. 88

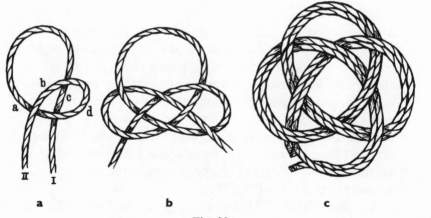

a   b   c

Fig. 89

over 'D' (Fig. 89b). *3.* Follow each end round the other's path once (as in figure 89*c*) or more often.

II. SENNITS

Sennit is a general term for braided ropes, in which the strands are plaited, not twisted, together. The commonest form, used for log lines, bell lanyards, better quality clothes lines, etc. is **Round Sennit,** which may be made from any even number of strands, although with six or more it will look better formed round a heart. This, however, has been omitted from figure 90 for easier illustration.

1. Whip the ends of the strands together. (It is possible to make a round sennit end to a laid rope by dividing the latter's strands into the number required. In this event put the whipping on the laid rope at the point where the sennit is to commence.) *2.* Cross each neighbouring pair of strands and, allowing the even-numbered to hang down, lift the odd-numbered up out of the way. In figure 90*a* the

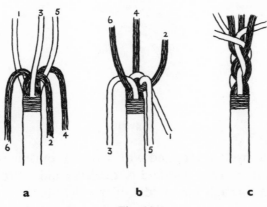

a   b   c

Fig. 90

even-numbered strands have gone to the right and the odd-
numbered to the left. They will continue to go in the same
directions. *3*. Pass each even-numbered strand over the odd-
numbered strand *to its right* and when this has been done,
hold the former up and allow the latter to drop down (Fig.
90*b*). *4*. Cross each odd-numbered strand over the even-
numbered *to its left*, hold it up and allow the even-numbered
to drop down. *5*. Repeat stages 3 and 4 alternately and the
result should be figure 90*c*. The process may sound complicated but in practice is very simple.

Square Sennit is made with eight, twelve or sixteen strands.
1. Divide the strands into two equal lots. *2*. Take one strand
from the right-hand lot and lead it round the back and
through the middle of the left-hand strands back to its own
lot, i.e. with eight strands it will pass outside two and inside
two of the left-hand strands (Fig. 91); with twelve, outside

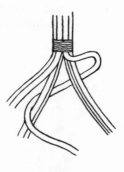

Fig. 91

three and inside three; and with sixteeen, outside four and
inside four. *3*. Take a strand of the left-hand lot round the
back and through the middle of the right-hand strands to
return to its own lot. *4*. Repeat stages 2 and 3 alternately,

using each strand in rotation. To begin with the sennit may be somewhat shapeless but after a few passes have been made it will tighten up.

Flat Sennit (Fig. 92). *1*. Secure the strands (any number) over a rope or bar. *2*. Bring the right-hand strand across to

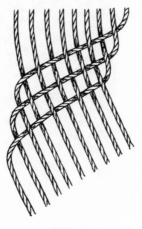

Fig. 92

the left passing it alternately under and over the other strands. *3*. Repeat stage 2, taking care to keep the sennit straight by slanting the other strands to the right.

French Sennit (Fig. 93). *1*. Start with an odd number of strands and divide them into two groups, one with one more strand than the other (the right-hand in the illustration). *2*. Work the outside strand of the larger group over and under its companions until it becomes the inside strand of the other group. (It goes from right to left in the illustration.) *3*. What was the smaller group is now the larger, so take its outside strand over and under its companions until

in its turn it becomes the inside strand of the other group.
4. Repeat stages 2 and 3 alternately.

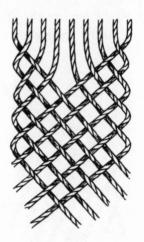

Fig. 93

Fig. 94

Common Sennit also requires an odd number of strands. *1.* Divide them into two groups, one with one more strand than the other. *2.* Bring the outside strand of the larger group across and add it to the smaller (which, of course, now becomes the larger). *3.* Repeat stage 2 *ad infinitum*. (Figure 94 shows Common Sennit being made with three strands.)

III. PLAITS

Plaits are allied to, but more complicated than, sennits. They may be made with one strand or with a number. The simplest single strand plait is the **Chain Plait.** *1.* At the end of the strand, make an Overhand Knot but use a small bight at the nearby end, instead of both ends. This will leave loop 'A' as in figure 95a. *2.* Through loop 'A' pull a small bight of the loose end 'B'. *3.* Through the new loop thus formed, pull another bight of the loose end and so on to

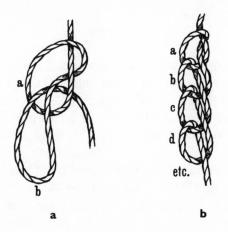

a   b

Fig. 95

make figure 95*b*. *4*. To finish, run the end through the last loop.

A Double Chain Plait is slightly more complicated. *1*. Form a Figure-of-Eight Knot but do not pull it tight (Fig. 96*a*). *2*. Dip the end I through the bight 'B'. This leaves a new bight under 'A'. *3*. Dip the end through the new bight. This leaves another new one under 'B'. *4*. Continue dipping

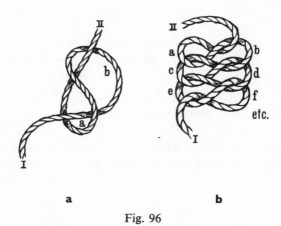

a   b

Fig. 96

the end through each new bight and finish by running the end through the last bight and hauling taut (Fig. 96*b*).

A Square Plait looks like a Square Sennit made with eight strands, but requires only one for its own manufacture. *1*. Make an Overhand Knot with the bight as in figure 97*a*. *2*. Pass the end I through the knot to make loop 'B'. *3*. Pass a bight of the end I through loop 'A' to make loop 'C' (Fig. 97*b*). *4*. Tighten loop 'A' by pulling on the upper side of loop 'B'. *5*. Pass I through loop 'B' to make loop 'D' (as 'C' was made in 'A'). *6*. Tighten loop 'B' by pulling on the upper side of loop 'C'. *7*. Continue passing a bight of the loose end alternately through loops to left and right and drawing the loops tight (Fig. 97c). *8.* To finish: pass the end through the last loop but one made, through the last loop, and down between the last two middle strands and haul taut.

Plaits can be made with three or more strands by repetition of some of the knots described earlier in this book.

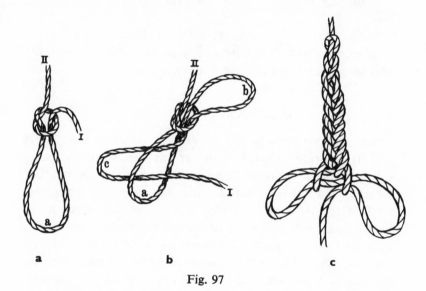

Fig. 97

Continuous Crowning, for instance, i.e. Crown Knots fashioned one after the other with the same strands, will produce a plait. If all the Crowns are made in the same direction, a spiral design is achieved; if alternately to right and left, a chain pattern. Continuous Wall Knotting will not produce a satisfactory plait unless made round a heart, but **Continuous Walling and Crowning,** i.e. Wall and Crown Knots alternating, will. So, too, will **Continuous Diamond**

and Crown Knotting, although this requires greater skill especially if using a number of strands.

An Overhand Knot Plait can be made with four, six or eight strands. Whip the ends of the strands together and number them in a circle. Then Overhand Knot pairs of strands in the following sequences:

With four strands: 1 with 3, 2 with 4; 1 with 3, 2 with 4, etc.

With six strands: 1 with 4; 2 with 5, 3 with 6, etc.

With eight strands: 1 with 4; 5 with 8; 2 with 7; 3 with 6; and so on, retaining the same sequence.

IV. COVERING A ROPE

There are two reasons for covering a rope: to protect it and to decorate it. For the former purpose, worming, parcelling and serving provide a general protection against the weather and normal wear and tear but if, in use, a rope is chafing against something else, additional safeguards may be needed, such as sword or thrum matting between the rope and a hard object. However, occasions arise when a rope—or even more likely a wire—may be rubbing against something softer than itself, in which event it is the latter that requires protection. Sails are, of course, an obvious example.

The best way, generally, to deal with this problem is to bind something relatively soft and yielding round the rope or wire. One material of ancient use for this is **Bag o' Wrinkle,** which is simply, if somewhat tediously, made. *1.* Seize together the ends of a long piece of small cordage and stretch it out, doubled. *2.* Insert a piece of wood to act as a spreader keeping the two parts away from each other. *3.*

Middle a thrum of some soft laid stuff across the two lines and pull its end up between them. *4.* Fill up the length of the lines with thrums so attached (Fig. 98).

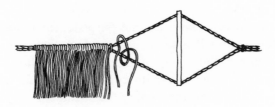

Fig. 98

Cockscombing can be both decorative and functional, e.g. on the Spindle Eye described in Chapter 5. With a single line it is simply Half Hitches put on alternately to right and left as in figure 99*a*. Greater protection and more elaborate decoration are gained by using more strands. *1.* Stopper

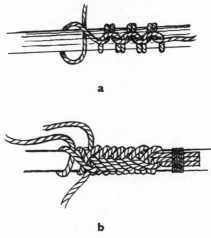

a

b

Fig. 99

these to the rope, ring or whatever it is that has to be covered. 2. With each strand in succession, form two Half Hitches, one towards, one away from the starting point and continue in this way, always taking that strand which is farthest back (Fig. 99*b*).

Pointing a Rope has a double purpose, for in addition to being the neatest it is also the soundest way of protecting a rope's end. *1*. Put a stop on the rope at a distance from its end equal to three times its circumference. *2*. Unlay the rope to the stop and then unlay the strands. *3*. Split a num-

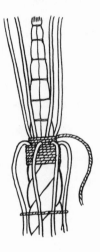

Fig. 100

ber of outside yarns and make an even number of nettles. *4*. Stop these nettles back on the standing part. *5*. Scrape the remaining yarns down to a tapering heart and marl them down very tightly with twine. *6*. Divide the nettles, laying every alternate one along the heart and allowing the others to drop down away from it. *7*. At the point where they divide into those going up and those down, bind on three turns of twine, and take a hitch with the last turn. *8*. Reverse the nettles, i.e. those that were up come down and *vice versa*. *9*. Take three more turns of twine and hitch (Fig. 100). *10*. Continue repeating stages 6 to 9 until the point has reached the desired length. *11*. Finish off by working a small eye in the end with nettles and yarns marled over with twine.

The rope need not end in an actual point; it can be a truncated cone, if wished. Moreover, the number and order of nettles taken up or down need not be as described above, which gives merely the simplest design. They can, for instance, be worked in groups of three or four, only one of which is taken up at a time whilst the others are held back, which will produce a spiral effect; and once you have grasped the underlying principles of pointing, there is no reason why you should not devise your own, individual pattern.

A number of variations can be achieved by working in various fancy knots; for instance, by starting with a Turk's Head (see below) over the stop you put on the strands at the point up to which they were unlaid, and by finishing with a Footrope Knot instead of a small eye. Diamond, Crown and Wall Knots can also be used, either singly or in combination, at either end of the point.

One method of making the point itself which does not employ the rope's own yarns, is to cover the heart with **Half Hitching.** *1*. Stop one end of the twine on the heart. *2*. With the other, make a series of Half Hitches round the last turn of the stopping, as shown in figure 101. *3*. Put on second, third fourth rows, etc. to cover the heart making each hitch through the bight of the Half Hitch above it in the preceding row.

Here again the point may be started with a fancy knot and the first row of Half Hitches made through its lowest turn. If Half Hitching is to look smart, however, it must be tightly made and it may be found that a needle is necessary to pass the end through tautly-hitched bights. The most satisfactory kind to use is a sailmaker's needle, complete with leather palm.

Fig. 101

Half Hitching is also suitable as a decorative—and to some extent protective—covering for bottles, jars and other cylindrical objects. On these it is probably better to start with a decorative knot or a length of tight chain plaiting in order to provide a firm base on which to 'anchor' the first row of hitches.

Another similar and simply made covering is **Spanish Hitching,** suitable for use with small cord, although unlike Half Hitching, it employs a number of separate strands, not one continuous piece. *1.* With the end of one strand— called the *warp*—middle a number of *hitching* strands around the rope or other object. *2.* Take the warp round again, a short distance below its first circuit and with each of the hitching strands make a round turn round it. *3*. Repeat stage 2 until the covering has reached the desired length. Various patterns are possible, depending upon the way the round turns are made. In figure 102 each of the hitching strands has been taken in the following way round the warp: outside, under, behind, over and to the right of its own standing part. They could be taken: behind, under, outside, over and down to the left of the standing part. Numerous other combinations will suggest themselves, but remember that whatever the pattern, it must repeat itself consistently.

Coach Whipping (or **Cross Pointing**) makes a very attractive covering with thin or thick strands or with strips of good cloth. It is a favourite design on telescopes, and is

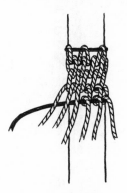

Fig. 102

suitable for any cylindrical object and for the middle or end of a rope. It requires an even number of strands—like Round Sennit, to which it is related—but these may consist of one, two, three or any number of individual parts. The illustrations show four strands, each doubled, in use, which is the maximum that one person can handle easily by himself. With more than that number, it is better to have an assistant to hold the strands already laid up in place whilst the cross pointing continues. With six strands the starting sequence would be: 1 over 2; 3 over 4; 5 over 6. With eight it would be the same plus 7 over 8. After that, every strand continues round in the direction in which it is already proceeding, passing alternately over and under its neighbours going the other way.

Thus, starting with four strands numbered in rotation figure 103 is obtained by passing: 1 over 2 and 3 over 4;

Fig. 103

4 over 1 and 2 over 3; 1 over 2 and 3 over 4. (Now 1 over 2 will complete the beginning of the next sequence.)

Continuous Crown, Wall and Diamond Knotting can each, individually or in combination with one of the others, be used to cover a rope. Stop the ends of the strands to the rope where the covering is to commence and then with them make a sequence of the chosen knots.

With the coverings described so far, there is no limit to the distance they may be carried from the starting point, although, of course, one will usually have been chosen beforehand. With the Pineapple Knot and a Herringbone Weave, however, the limits are fixed at the very beginning.

A **Pineapple Knot** makes a very attractive raised handle on a rope or covering for a bump such as is formed by a Shroud Knot or Short Splice. *1.* Provide a smooth covering to the Shroud Knot or, if this is to be merely a handle, raise a 'mouse' on the rope, by winding on marline or yarns. *2.* Stick two pieces of cord long enough to make the knot through the 'mouse' at one end—use a pricker of some sort to do it—at right angles to each other. *3.* Put a light whipping on them and crown them as shown in figure 104*a*. *4.* Take the four ends of cord spirally down to the other end of the 'mouse' and whip them temporarily. *5.* Crown the ends upwards right handed (Fig. 104*b*). *6.* Work the cords back to the top of the 'mouse' by tucking each alternately under and over the strands of the spiral already

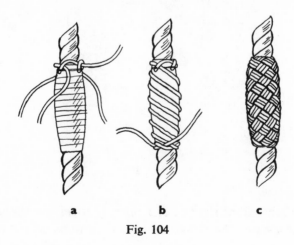

a   b   c

Fig. 104

put on, in the opposite direction to the spiral. You now have two spirals interlocking and the whippings may be cut off *7*. Follow round until the 'mouse' is closely covered (Fig. 104*c*). This knot makes a form of cross-pointing and three or more cords can be used if desired.

Herringbone Weave. *1*. Lay six or eight long strands along the rope, etc. and seize them at either end of the space to be covered. *2*. Skew them diagonally so that they run at an angle of 45 degrees to the run of the rope. *3*. Tuck the lower ends up and to the right over and under until they reach the rim of the weave. *4*. Tuck the upper ends down and to the left similarly. This will make the right-going diagonals double whilst those to the left have remained single as in figure 105*a*. *5*. Continue tucking both sets of ends; when at the top, down and to the left; when at the bottom, up and to the right; over and under until the weave is completed as in figure 105*b*. *6*. To finish off: scatter the ends well,

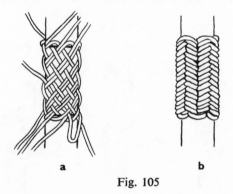

a   b

Fig. 105

tuck them out of sight after trimming them, cut the seizings and draw out the weave evenly. Variations to the pattern can be achieved by taking ends over two and under two, over two and under three and so on (but be consistent!).

The Turk's Head. The popularity of this design undoubtedly entitles it to its own separate section. Turk's Heads with a rope's strands are simply made, as described in Chapter 4, but when using only a single strand they can become considerably more complicated.

A Turk's Head is always made *round* something, and if we think of this object as being the axis of the knot, we can describe the latter by its number of parts and turns.

The parts of a Turk's Head: Draw a line parallel to the axis across the knot in its completed first stage, i.e. before any following-round has begun, and the number of strands that it crosses is the number of parts of the knot. Later, when the knot has been doubled or trebled, such a line will cut two or three times as many strands, but this does not alter the number of parts.

The turns of a Turk's Head: Again in the completed first stage, the number of times the rope moves from one side of the knot to the other *and back* in tracing its path round, is the number of turns.

To make a three-part, four-turn Turk's Head, which is the simplest design. *1.* Make a loose Stunsail Halyard Bend as in figure 106*a*. *2.* Push the right-hand bight 'A' to the left and the left-hand bight 'B' to the right over 'A'. *3.* Take the end I over 'B' and under 'A' (Fig. 106*b*). This completes the first stage except that the bends and crossings of the rope should be evened out to make the knot symmetrical *4.* Follow round once or twice.

To increase the number of turns (but not of parts) after stage 3 push bight 'A' to the right and 'B' to the left and tuck the end I again, but to the right; then repeat stages 2 and 3. The larger the circumference of the object, the more turns will be needed to cover it effectively and the 'increasing' process can be repeated as often as necessary before commencing the following round. As with many things practical experiment is the best teacher.

a   b

Fig. 106

To make a four-part Turk's Head: *1.* Make an Overhand Knot as in figure 107*a*. *2.* Carry the end I round to pass under at 'A' and 'B' as shown in figure 107*b*. *3.* Carry the

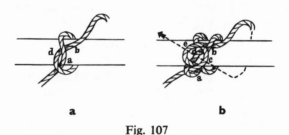

a   b

Fig. 107

end I round again to pass over at 'C', under at 'D' and over at 'E'. *4.* Follow round once or twice.

To make more complicated knots, especially if they are to be long ones, the simpler way is to use either studs or a 'former'. As the studs have to be driven into the object to be covered, this precludes their use on metal, but a 'former' can be used on an object of any material.

To make a Turk's Head using studs.[1] *1.* At either end of the area to be covered, drive in one stud for each of the turns it is desired to incorporate into the Turk's Head. The studs should be equally spaced and each should have its 'opposite number' at the other end of the knot and on the opposite side of the object (see figure 108). *2.* Start at any stud at the left-hand end and make spiral turns to reach its 'opposite number' stud at the other end. *3.* Take the rope round this stud and make a similar number of spiral turns back towards the start but, if you are using an uneven number of studs at either end, make this return spiral pass alternately over and under the strands of the first spiral where it crosses them (Fig. 108). If you have an even number of studs at

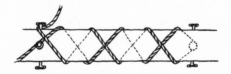

Fig. 108

either end, make a succession of 'over' crossings. *4.* Take the rope past the 'starting' stud and round the one beyond it. *5.* Make the same number of spiral turns as previously to the next 'opposite number' stud at the other end of the knot, passing *over* where the preceding turn passed under, and *under* where it passed over. *6.* Take the rope round the 'opposite number' stud, as in stage 3, and make spiral turns back to the start, again passing over or under in contrast to the position of the preceding turn. *7.* Continue in this fashion from one end of the knot to the other until all the studs have been used, when the first stage will have

[1]As devised by Captain E. W. Denison, R.N.

been completed. *8.* Follow round once, twice or more often to complete the covering.

Using a Former to make a Turk's Head[1] has the advantage that the knot can be made round an object of any material, including metal, since the pins are driven into a quite separate piece of wood. This is the *former*, a board which rarely needs to be more than 4 in. square and on which can be fashioned a Turk's Head of almost any complexity, with the valuable added attractions that all the tucks are made on the same side of the object so that there is no need to keep turning it over or moving round to the back; that it is easier to remember where to make the tucks; and that the tucks, when made, hold themselves in place. To use a 'former':

1. On the planking, set up two parallel rows of six or seven pegs or pins each as in figure 109*a*. (They have to be withdrawn later, so do not drive them in too tightly.) *2.* Lash the former to the object to be covered very securely, with the rows of pins at right angles to its axis as in figure 109*a*. *3.* Lay the standing end of the cord in front of Left Hand No. 1 pin and take the working end round Right Hand No. 1 and then across diagonally between the two rows of pins. *4.* Bring the working end round under the object and up on the near side of the 'former', over the standing end and round Left Hand No. 1. *5.* Take the working end across to Right Hand No. 2 crossing the first diagonal strand (a) *over* if you are using an even number of pins on either side; or (b) *under* if you are using an uneven number (Fig. 109*b*). *6.* Bring the working end round under to the near side and tuck it under and over to Left Hand No. 2 pin. *7.* Continue to pass the working end from left to

[1]As devised by Mr John Alexander and described in *Knots, Splices and Fancy Work*, by Charles L. Spencer (Dodd, Mead and Company, 1942).

right and then round under to the near side, i.e. from Left
Hand No. 2 to Right Hand No. 3 to Left Hand No. 3 to
Right Hand No. 4, etc. passing it either over or under each
strand it crosses in the opposite way to that in which the
previous turn crossed that strand. Generally this means that
the working end simply goes under and over successive
strands but occasionally you will find that you have to

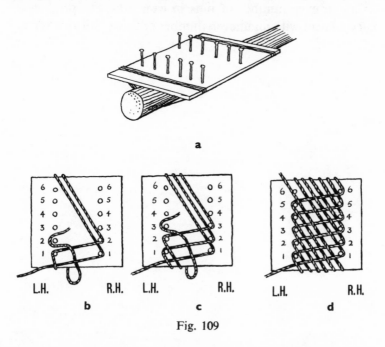

Fig. 109

make two successive 'overs' to fit in with the lay of the
previous turn. Thus in figure 109c the end has passed over,
under, *over* to Left Hand No. 3 pin and will now have to go
over again, then under and over to Right Hand No. 4
because the previous turn went under turn I.

When the working end has reached the last left-hand pin

as in figure 109*d*, the knot is complete, ready for doubling. The pins are now removed, the lashings which hold the 'former' to the object are cut, and the 'former' is slid out, leaving the knot loosely, but correctly woven, round the object. All that remains is to double or treble it if desired and to work it tight. In description, the process may seem complicated but it is fairly straightforward in practice. Using an even number of pins in each row will produce a Turk's Head with an uneven number of turns and vice versa.

CHAPTER EIGHT

Blocks and tackles

I. BLOCKS

The Parts of a Block.

1. *The shell* is the outside case.

2. *The sheave* is the grooved wheel over which the rope travels. It is made of phosphor bronze, iron or lignum vitae, a self-lubricating, very hard wood which makes the best sheave but will be scored if used with a wire rope. *A roller sheave* has metal rollers fitted to the bush that work round the sheave pin. In some blocks ball bearings are used for the same purpose.

3. *The bush* is the metal centre of the sheave through which the pin passes.

4. *The sheave pin* is the axle on which the sheave revolves. It is a steel pin that passes through the shell and from time to time should be punched out with a spike and greased with blacklead and tallow or solid Vaseline.

5. *The crown* is the top of the block.

6. *The tail* is the bottom of the block.

7. *The swallow* is the opening between the cheeks of the shell through which the rope passes.

8. *The cheeks* are the sides of the shell on each side of the swallow.

9. *The score* is a groove on the outside of a wooden block to take a rope strop and it is deeper at the tail than at the crown. Some blocks have two scores to take a double strop. Some, known as **Iron Bound Blocks,** are fitted with a heavy iron strop, instead of one of rope or wire. An **Internal Iron Bound Block** has a removable forked shape iron strop

inserted down through either side of the shell, often with one fork longer than the other so that it projects as a lug to which the standing end of the tackle may be shackled.

Clump blocks, somewhat out of date nowadays, are very round, squat blocks cut from a single piece of wood. **Swivel blocks** are fitted with a swivel hook or eye at the crown so that they may slew if necessary without twisting the ropes rove through them.

A snatch block has a portion of the shell near the crown cut away on one side and covered with a hinged clamp, which is kept in place with a split pin or spring. This allows the middle of a rope to be placed over the sheave without the necessity of reeving the end through the swallow (Fig. 111).

A Non-toppling block is a type used mainly on lifeboat falls. Its tail is decidedly heavier than its crown so that it always stays crown upwards. It has no connexion with a **Tail Block,** which is simply a common block with a tail of rope instead of an eye, hook or shackle at the crown (Fig. 113).

Sister blocks and **fiddle blocks** are rarely found outside yachts. They are both double blocks with the sheaves arranged vertically one over the other instead of side by side, in order to save space. In a sister block the sheaves are of the same size; in a fiddle block the upper is larger than the lower in order to prevent the rope passing over it from chafing against that passing over its partner. Both types of block are nowadays internally iron bound and usually fitted with a hook at the crown and a becket at the tail.

To fit a strop to a block: *1.* Make a grommet of rope or wire long enough to pass round the block and the thimble which is to be secured to its crown (or possibly, round a spar to which the block is to be semi-permanently secured.

2. Worm, parcel and serve the grommet and, to make a really first-class job of it, sew on tightly a leather jacket over the serving. *3.* Place the block and thimble inside the strop and secure the whole by both ends, either vertically or horizontally, so that everything is held in position. *4.* Put a tight Round Seizing on the two parts of the strop between the thimble (or spar) and the block (Fig. 110).

Fig. 110

To fit a double strop to a block: *1.* Make a grommet as in stage 1 above, but of double the length. *2.* Double it into two equal bights and seize them at the crown. *3.* Carry out stages 3 and 4 as above, except that there will be four parts of the strop to seize, not two.

II. TACKLES

Blocks have two different functions. One is to alter the direction of a rope so that it can be led to a winch or to a place where a man can haul on it more easily. Almost any type of block can be used thus as a **Leading Block,** but remember that it will have to be fixed, by a shackle, hook, hitch or splice, firmly enough to take the strain that will come on it (Fig. 111).

(The most unusual tug-of-war contest I ever took part in —unsuccessfully, I regret to add—made ingenious use of leading blocks. The venue was the fore part of a relatively

Fig. 111

small warship from whose forecastle, cluttered with anchors, cables, etc., a narrow strip of deck led aft on either side of the superstructure. There seemed scarcely room to swing a cat, let alone stage a tug-of-war, but a long rope was led from one strip of deck, on to the forecastle, through two leading blocks set athwartship, and aft along the other strip. Competing teams manned opposite ends of the rope. They could not see each other and they both pulled in the same direction, aft! Nevertheless, it was genuine tug-of-war and the arrangement could be adapted for the same purpose anywhere space is restricted.)

The lifting power of tackles

The second function of blocks is to combine with one another to form tackles, or purchases, which will increase the lifting or hauling power of your arm, capstan, winch, windlass, etc. In all tackles except the Single Whip—which offers merely a more convenient hauling position but no gain in power—at least one block moves with the load, and the power ratio of any tackle is the number of parts of rope at this block. Where a rope enters a block is counted as one part, where it leaves as another; and if the standing end of the rope is secured to the moving block, that also counts as one part.

Types of Purchase

1. **Single whip.** A rope rove through a single fixed block with one end as the hauling part and the other as the

Fig. 112

standing end secured to the load to be lifted. Power gained: nil.

2. **Double whip** (Fig. 112). Power gained: double.

3. **Gun tackle.** Two single blocks with the standing end of

the rope made fast to one. Power gained: double; or three times if the standing end block is the moving one.

4. **Watch or Luff Tackle.** A double block and a single to which the standing end is secured. Power gained: three times; or four if the double block moves.

5. **Jigger or Handy Billy** (Fig. 113). This is a Luff Tackle

Fig. 113

but the double block has a tail instead of a hook for securing on another rope as shown in the illustration. It is often used to obtain greater hauling power on another purchase.

6. **A Runner.** This, always used in conjunction with another purchase, is like a single whip but gives doubled power

because the block moves, the standing end of the fall being made fast to the deck, a beam or some other place.

7. **A Double Luff Tackle.** Two double blocks. Power gained: four or five times.

8. **Three and Two Tackle.** A double and a treble block. Power gained: five or six times.

9. **A Threefold Purchase.** Two treble blocks. Power gained: six or seven times.

Fourfold purchases (i.e. two four-fold blocks) and over are used only on the very heaviest derricks and cranes.

Because of friction in the working parts of the blocks, not all the power stated above is actually gained and ten per cent should be added to the load for every sheave in the purchase in calculating the strength of rope required. Thus if an object weighing, say, 300 lb. is to be hoisted by a Gun Tackle, then its weight must be taken as 300 lb. plus twice one-tenth of that weight, equals 360 lb. A Gun Tackle, rigged with the standing part of the rope at the top, gives double power. The load on the fall, or hauling part of the tackle, will therefore be 180 lb. Double this for safety— the regulations in docks regarding the handling of cargo demand quadrupling it—and you find that you need a rope with a breaking strength of not less than 360 lb. Thus a standard grade 1-in. manila will be adequate.

At the standing end of the tackle, however, the stress put on is equal to the weight lifted plus the load on the hauling part; or in the example above, 300 lb. plus 180 lb., equals 480 lb. At least doubling this shows that if, for some reason, you intend lashing your top block to a girder or spar, a standard grade 1-in. manila will be scarcely sufficient for safety.

Looking at the question of friction from another angle, the ten per cent can be subtracted from the total load your tackle will bear. Thus the lifting capacity of a Luff Tackle rigged with 1½-in. Nylon is not 5,000 lb. multiplied by three, equals 15,000 lb., but 15,000 lb. less three times ten per cent which gives 13,500 lb. The safe working load is therefore 6,750 lb. at which the load on the standing end of the tackle would be 6,750 + (6,750 ÷ 3) lb., equals 9,000 lb. The latter is the load which the shackle, hook or rope that secures the standing block must be capable of *safely* sustaining if you use your tackle to its safe limit.

PART TWO

STEEL WIRE ROPE

CHAPTER NINE

The construction and care of wire ropes

I. TYPES OF WIRE ROPE

BECAUSE steel wire rope is a non-natural fabricated product, it lends itself far more than hempen rope to specialized constructions designed to meet particular needs. One leading manufacturing firm lists forty-one different cross-sections in its catalogue and yet apologizes that limitations of space prohibit reference to all possible rope constructions. Moreover, for each cross-section showing a particular arrangement of strands, a number of different ropes are produced varying in size, quality of metal and treatment, e.g. whether they have been galvanized or not.

Obviously then this book, which is also limited for space, cannot deal with every make of wire rope so that, if, as is rather unlikely, you intend installing a large passenger lift, erecting a giant crane or towing a battleship to a breaker's yard, you would be advised to make your inquiries directly of a manufacturer, for below we deal only with ropes likely to be of use in yachting and other recreations and hobbies. These all come into the category known as **round strand ropes.**

They are given this name because they all consist of strands round in cross-section, made up of long threads of steel (wires) which are also round in section. The number of strands is usually six, laid up right-handed round a fibre heart, but exceptions exist where eight strands are twisted round a fibre heart and others where six encircle a core which, is in effect, a smaller wire rope on its own account (Figs. 114*a* and *b*).

Unlike the yarns in a hempen rope which are of a standard thickness, the threads which make up the strands of wire rope vary considerably in diameter. The size of a rope—which, as with hempen ropes, is the measurement of its circumference—is increased without altering the arrangement of its strands by thickening the wires of which they are composed. This, naturally, increases its weight as well as its breaking strength. On the other hand, a rope with a greater number of threads per strand will, in general, be stronger than another of the same size but with a lesser number of threads, without being correspondingly heavier. It will also be more flexible, a quality which is further increased if every strand, as well as the rope itself, is twisted round a fibre heart (Fig. 114*b*).

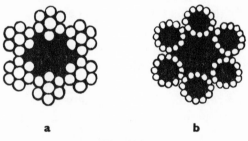

a   b

Fig. 114

Usually the threads have a left-handed twist in contrast to the right-hand run of the strands and a rope so constructed is said to have an **Ordinary** (or **Regular**) **Lay**; but sometimes the threads have the same twist as the strands. This construction, known as **Lang's Lay,** offers a better wearing surface when in use but should only be installed by an expert and not employed where there is any danger of the load being allowed to rotate.

The easiest wire for a novice to handle is one with a **Pre-formed** or **True Lay.** In this rope the threads and strands are shaped, before laying up, to the helix they will require in the completed rope. This is said to make the rope more resistant to kinking, to give it a longer life and to place a more balanced load on the strands, but perhaps its greatest attraction is that the strands do not fly apart when cut. In wire rope of normal construction the strands, and the threads within the strands, are like steel springs under tension so that unless the end of the rope is whipped they will separate, often violently. As we shall see in the next chapter, this poses certain problems in splicing, which would not be encountered with pre-formed rope.

Further, when a thread in the latter breaks, it lies flat. It neither thrusts into adjacent wires, thus damaging them, nor does it project outward like a needle ready to dig into any unwary hand sliding along the rope. This is a tremendous boon in any wire that is constantly handled, for projecting ends can be extremely dangerous, so much so that it is advisable to wear leather gloves when working with wire of normal lay.

However, the nicest wire of all to handle is the combined steel and fibre rope in which the strands not only encircle the rope's fibre heart, and are themselves laid up round their own individual hearts but are also completely covered with fibre, usually manila. Thus only fibre appears on the outside of the rope, which makes it easier and safer to grip and gives it a better hold, especially when wet, around a capstan or winch drum.

11. UNCOILING AND COILING

It is even more important when using wire rope than it is with hempen to prevent kinks developing, if only because it is the devil's own job to take them out once they have formed; although, of course, their effect upon the life and strength of the rope is equally important. **Opening a new coil** therefore demands the greatest care and a wire rope should always be unwound in the opposite direction to which it was made up.

If the rope is light and flexible, the coil can be rolled open along the ground or deck in the same way that a fireman lays out a hose (Fig. 115).

Fig. 115

If it is too heavy or inflexible for this treatment, it must be held still and rotated as the wire is taken off, always from the outside. (Never start with the inside end.) Just how this is to be done depends upon whether the rope arrives packed in a coil or on a reel. If the latter, pass a shaft through the reel and place it on standards as in figure 116. Then cut the outside lashings only and haul off the rope, applying some form of brake to the reel to ensure that the rope never slackens.

A coil, on the other hand, needs to be lashed down on to some form of turntable with two strong battens secured crosswise on top of it to prevent any turns from springing off and kinking. The turntable, like the reel mentioned above, should be braked to keep the rope tight.

Fig. 116

If no turntable is available, lash two substantial pieces of wood together to form a cross and secure two bridles of strong rope to them, with the four ropes' ends each fastened securely to a separate leg about half-way between its end

Fig. 117

and the centre of the cross. These bridles should be long enough for their bights to reach up through the middle of the coil when it is laid on the cross. Now hook a tackle or crane wire on to the bridle, hoist the coil far enough to allow it to revolve freely and proceed as for using a turntable (Fig. 117), remembering to keep the wire taut as you haul it off. If the tackle or crane hook is of the swivel variety, so much the better, for it will revolve with the coil whilst the crane wire or tackle will remain stationary. If it is not, after every few revolutions the coil must be lowered and unhooked in order to take the turns out of the tackle. A wire rope packed on a reel can also be run off by this method if no shaft or standards are available.

Stowing a wire when you have finished with it is just as important a task to do correctly as breaking open a new coil. If the rope is not too long or large, it may be coiled by hand; in a clockwise direction if it has a right-handed lay, anti-clockwise if left-handed; and the coil should be firmly stopped in at least three places with spunyarn or other small cord in order to prevent the turns springing off. If the rope is large and/or long, it should be wound on to a reel and its outer end lashed down. A wire rope thrown down higgledy-piggledy will almost certainly develop kinks.

Because a wire rope not in use is better kept on a reel, when a length is being taken off a new coil for a particular purpose, measure carefully what you will require and then add on 18 in. to 2 ft. for each splice you intend making, e.g. you may intend putting an eye in one or both ends.

III. Cutting a Wire Rope

Having decided where you want to cut the rope, put a stout yarn whipping on either side of that point. *This is essential* for all wire ropes except those with a pre-formed lay, for if you do not do it, as soon as you cut through the strands they will fly apart and you will not be able to lay them up properly again.

Scissors and knives are useless for cutting wire ropes; for that task you need a hammer and a cold chisel. To obtain a firm, even cut: lay the rope on some solid foundation of metal or stone (wood is too soft); then flatten the surface between the whippings with a few sharp blows from the edge of the hammer; and finally hammer the chisel through the flattened part.

Lastly, to obtain the longest possible service from your wire ropes oil them occasionally and do not run them through blocks that are too small.

Oiling lubricates and protects the strands. The particular dressing to be applied will depend upon how the rope was treated during manufacture and advice should be sought of the manufacturer or supplier. Galvanized ropes do not need oiling to the same extent as non-galvanized although they will last longer if so treated, but since in a yacht's rigging oiled ropes are likely to leave some most unsightly stains on the sails, yachtsmen prefer to rely solely upon the galvanizing to protect the steel wires from the attacks of rain and sea water. The same consideration applies wherever else a wire rope comes into contact with cloth, e.g. in the cord through the top of a tennis net.

However, if the yachtsman lays his boat up for the winter, a thin coating of Vaseline on all his wire ropes will help to lengthen their lives. It can be wiped off easily in the spring. A more permanent alternative is to clean the ropes thoroughly and apply a coating of marine varnish.

A very satisfactory alternative to oiling or galvanizing is the modern plastic covering of wire ropes. Ropes so covered, however, are extremely difficult to splice and if fittings such as eyes are required on them, putting them there is a factory job; but the factory will gauge the fitting to the rope, making a seal which will have greater strength than any splice.

Those whose acquaintance with galvanizing is confined to objects such as dustbins, on which the zinc coating is relatively thick, must remember that on steel wire ropes it is very thin and can easily be knocked off by running the ropes through blocks whose sheaves are either too rough-surfaced or too small. Therefore smooth sheaves surfaces with emery paper and always use adequately sized blocks.

The minimum size of block to use for different ropes is given in the following table:

Circumference of rope	*Under 2″*	*2″*	*2¼″*	*2½″*	*2¾″*	*3″*
Minimum outside diameter of sheave	10″	12″	14″	14″	16″	16″

IV. Breaking Strengths of Galvanized Marine Steel Wire Ropes

Size (dia.)	Non-flexible	Ordinary flexible		Special flexible	Extra special flexible
	(6 strands 7 wires/ 1 fibre core)	(6 strands/ 12 wires/ 7 fibre cores)	(6 strands/ 19 wires/ 1 fibre core)	(6 strands/ 24 wires/ 7 fibre cores)	(6 strands/ 37 wires/ 1 fibre core)
in.	tons	tons	tons	tons	tons
⅛	·54	·36	·53	—	—
³⁄₁₆	1·14	·72	1·06	.93	—
¼	1·97	1·27	2·05	1.58	1·93
⁵⁄₁₆	3·05	1·94	3·18	3.95*	3·33
⁷⁄₁₆	5·91	3·76	6·17	—	5·83
½	7·68	4·91	8·91	6.96	7·59
⁹⁄₁₆	9·68	6·18	10·12	10.77‡	9·60
⅝	11·92	7·61	12·43	—	11·75
¾	16·97	10·87	17·74	15.44	16·80
1	29·57	19·07	31·20	27.18	29·66

*Diameter: ⅜ in.
‡Diameter: ⅝ in.

Notes: (a) The number of wires quoted in each column refers to the number in each strand, so that extra special flexible steel wire rope contains, all told, 222 wires.

(b) Ropes having seven-fibre cores have a core inside each strand as well as one centrally in the rope.

(c) Two standards of the 6/19/1, 6/24/7 and 6/37/1 ropes are made. The figures quoted are for the one with the lower breaking strength.

(d) A rough and ready rule for finding the breaking strength of flexible steel wire rope is to square its circumference and multiply by two. The answer is the breaking strength in tons.

(e) Ropes larger than 1 in. diameter are unlikely to be used by many readers of this book and figures for these are therefore not quoted.

The relative strengths of various ropes

To enable a quick, approximate comparison to be made between the breaking strengths and weights of various types of rope, the table below shows the smallest size required for a particular load, based on the principle that no rope should be used under a strain equal to more than half its breaking strength. The weights given are in every case for 100 feet of rope.

ROPE REQUIRED TO LIFT A GIVEN LOAD

Load (tons)	Standard Manila		Nylon and Goldline		Dacron		Steel Wire Rope 6/19/1		6/24/7	
	Size in. (circ.)	Wt. lbs.	Size in. (circ.)	Wt. lbs.	Size in. (circ.)	Wt. lbs.	Size in. (diam.)	Wt. lbs.	Size in. (diam.)	Wt. lbs.
1	2	13·1	1⅛	3·85	1¼	6·6	¼	10	$\frac{5}{16}$	12·8
2	3	26·5	1¾	8·65	2	12·8	⅜	23	$\frac{7}{16}$	26·0
3	3½	35·2	2¼	15·5	2¼	18·0	$\frac{7}{16}$	31	½	35
5	5	73.0	2¾	20·8	3	30·0	$\frac{9}{16}$	51	⅝	54
10	7	143·0	3¾	38·0	5	84·0	$\frac{13}{16}$	107	⅞	106
20	11	360·0	5½	84·0	7	163.0	1¼	250	1¼	216

CHAPTER TEN

Wire splicing

I. General Remarks

The tools needed for wire splicing are:
Hammer
Tucker for splicing small strands
Round marline-spike
Cold chisel
Pair of steel wire cutters
Vice
Flat marline-spike
Serving mallet, preferably one with a small reel attached
to the handle to hold seizing wire

This list gives the ideal; the reality often falls short of it;
but the hammer, chisel and round spike are essential whilst
it is possible to splice only small wires without a vice, and
even then the job is easier with one.

One other 'tool' deserves mention although it is, in fact,
a substitute for splicing, not an aid to it. This is the **Wire
Rope Clip.** For some reason this is rarely referred to in books
on wire splicing, perhaps because its use is frowned upon
by purists, but from my experience three such clips will hold
two wires together very efficiently. (See figure 118 for their
use in forming an eye.) Their great attraction is that it takes

Fig. 118

only a few minutes to screw three on with a wrench where a splice might take half an hour or more; their drawback is that they are ugly and cannot be used on a wire that has to reeve through a block or pass round a winch drum.

Worming, parcelling and serving are used on wire ropes, and particularly on splices, for the same reasons that they are used on hempen, and they are put on in the same way. However, instead of spunyarn, **Seizing Wire** is often put on for the serving. This is a very thin, flexible seven-ply, galvanized wire, of six strands twisted round a seventh that forms the heart, made in various sizes from one-sixteenth to one-eighth inches. As well as for serving, it is also used for seizings, such as are described in Chapter 6, or any other form of binding on wire rope, but it should not be used on hempen.

Because seizing wire is small to hold and often greasy, it is sometimes difficult to pull tight. A Marline Hitch should NOT be used to obtain a better purchase as it will probably damage the seizing wire. Instead, lay the handle of a hammer, near the head, across the hauling part of the wire and take a round turn with its loose end between the hammer head and the hauling part. Now hold the loose end against the handle and you can take a good pull without fear of the wire slipping, for the hauling part will jam the loose end against the hammer head. (It is a form of Blackwall Hitch.)

It will often be found more convenient to work on a splice if the wire is suspended horizontally at about chest height but, especially if the wire is a large one, the first round of tucks should be made with it held securely in a vice. It is often easier to drive a spike through a wire if the latter is resting on something solid.

When tucking one strand under another, try to avoid distorting their natural lay by tucking the end too close to the point where it emerges from under the previous strand. It is better to pass the spike under the strand where the tuck is to be made and then work it down the wire for a few inches with a spiral movement. Now pass the end through and work the spike back to its original position, at the same time pulling the strand through, remove the spike and complete the job of pulling the strand tight. In any case, in wire splicing, never remove the spike from under a strand before you have passed the end through, even though in splicing hempen rope you can force a strand through without, perhaps, using a spike at all.

After making the first round of tucks, some people hold all the ends together along the standing part and beat the splice with a spike to make everything tight. This should not be done with any succeeding tucks, nor should the strands be hammered back as far as they will go. Rather, the second and following tucks should be allowed to lie in a long natural lay without being in any way loose.

In any splice, the end of the rope must be unlaid to a certain point in order to provide ends long enough to make the necessary tucks. With a hempen rope, a whipping at this point is not always necessary; with a wire rope it is *essential*. It should be about 2 in. long, made with rope yarn or, better still, marline, and should be put on *away* from the end of the rope. (A West Country Whipping will probably be found to be the easiest to make.)

Before cutting the whipping at the end of the rope and allowing the strands to unlay to the new one you have put on, however, put another light seizing about 8 in. from the end, unlay only to this and then whip the end of each individual strand. If this is not done, each strand will open out and unlay when the end whipping is cut. Once the strand whippings are on, the temporary seizing can be removed.

With the strands apart and whipped individually, cut out the rope's fibre heart as far back as possible. If the strands have individual hearts, these, too, can be cut out one at a time, removing each whipping as needed and replacing it before you move on to the next strand. Cutting out the strand hearts is not essential, but it leads to a slimmer, neater and perhaps safer splice.

Lastly, do not be niggardly in the length you allow in ends for tucking. Short ends are harder to grip and bend. Two feet should be sufficient for anything up to a 3-in. rope.

II. EYE SPLICES

To turn in a thimble. If the eye is to contain a thimble, lay the grooved part of the latter on the rope with its fork on the whipping which holds the unlaid strands. Then turn it over along the rope once and mark where the fork now is. Between this point and the whipping will be the portion of rope that encloses the thimble and this should be served. Now secure the crown of the thimble exactly to the centre of the serving and, when it is fast, bend the rope round it in the form of a loop, using the jaws of a vice to squeeze it into shape if it is a large rope. Finally seize both sides of the thimble between the crown and the fork, to the rope to hold it in place. (This whole operation can be performed *before* the end whipping is cut and the strands unlaid, but not before the whipping up to which they will be unlaid has been put on.)

The inclusion or otherwise of a thimble makes no difference to the tucking.

To make a left-handed (naval) Splice. (In this splice and in those that follow, the ends are numbered in Arabic numerals and the strands under which they are tucked in

Roman. In every case the numbering is as follows: When the unlaid ends are spread out evenly in natural order, the end on the extreme right is No. 1. Then, reading to the left, come Nos. 2, 3, 4, 5 and 6, the extreme left-hand end. When

Turning in a thimble on a small wire.
Fig. 119

these ends are laid on the standing part of the rope with their fork at the point where the splice is to commence, the strand nearest to end No. 1 is strand I. Then, reading to the left round the rope, come strands II, III, IV, V and VI which is I's right-hand neighbour.)

1. Tuck end No. 1 under strand I, 2 under II, 3 under III, and 4 under IV, all tucks to be made from right to left. *2.* Tuck end No. 6 under strands V and VI. *3.* Pull out the spike only far enough to allow strand VI to drop down and tuck end No. 5 under strand V. Every end now passes under its own strand except end No. 6 which passes under *two* strands, from right to left like the others. *4.* Haul and beat the tucks tight (Fig. 120*a*). This completes the first set of tucks.

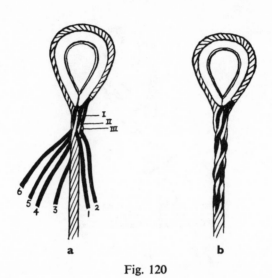

Fig. 120

Some people cut the strand hearts out now instead of before making the first tucks. A good rope yarn whipping may also be put over the completed tucks before proceeding to stage 5 in order to hold them in place whilst completing the splice.

5. Tuck all ends again twice, over one, under one, as in splicing hempen rope. *6.* Lay back one-third of each end along the wire, stop these portions and make another set of tucks with the remaining two-thirds. *7.* Similarly lay back and stop a second third and tuck the remainder of each strand. This tapers the splice off neatly (Fig. 120*b*). Cut off all ends and serve over the splice.

To make a right-handed Eye Splice. This splice, sometimes called 'over and under' or 'Liverpool style', is popular in the merchant marine for it is quicker to make than a left-handed splice; but its use is frowned upon in the navy because it is not so strong. In any case, it should never be used on a wire that is liable to spin, e.g. in hoisting, as it might unlay.

1. Tuck end No. 1 under strands II and I (in that order) *from left to right. 2.* Drop strand I off the point of the spike and tuck end No. 2 under strand II *from left to right. 3.* Tuck ends Nos. 3, 4, 5 and 6 also from left to right under III, IV, V and VI respectively. This completes the first set of tucks. *4.* Tuck again three times with full strands and twice with 'thirded' from left to right so that each end is always tucked under the same strand (in other words, so that it encircles it spirally). *5.* Cut off ends and serve.

To make a left-handed Locking Splice. As its name implies, this splice contains a 'lock' which helps to prevent the splice from drawing. *1.* Tuck end No. 1 under strand I *from left to right. 2.* Tuck end No. 2 under strand II *from right to left. 3.* Keeping the spike still under strand II, take end No. 6 underneath everything and tuck it under strand II *from left to right.* This makes the cross or lock. *4.* Tuck end No. 3 under strand III *from right to left. 5.* Tuck end No. 5 under strands IV and V *from right to left. 6.* Drop strand V off the point of the spike and tuck end No. 4 under strand IV from right to left. This completes the first set of tucks. *7.* Continue as for a simple left-handed splice with all tucks over one, under one, from right to left.

To make a 3, 2 and 1 Splice. This is another easily made, but not quite so strong, splice. *1.* Without injuring the fibre heart, insert the spike through the rope, entering between strands III and IV and emerging between strands I and VI.

2. Pass end No. 1 through beside the spike, on the opposite side of it to the heart, which should be to the left of the spike. *3.* Drop strand I off the spike point and pass end No. 2 through to emerge between I and II. *4.* Drop strand II off the point and pass end No. 3 through to emerge between II and III. Three ends now enter through the centre but emerge from under different strands. *5.* Tuck 4 under IV, 5 under V and 6 under VI all from left to right. *6.* Continue as for a right-handed splice.

To make a Reduced Eye Splice. If, for some reason, an ordinary eye splice will be too bulky, a reduced splice might serve instead, but it is not, of course, so strong. *1.* Measure off enough rope to make an eye of the required size, plus the length of ends needed to make four tucks, and pass a stout whipping round it at this point. *2.* Unlay to this point and halve every strand and the heart. *3.* Re-lay six half strands (one from each whole strand) and half of the heart to form a reduced wire and proceed as for a normal eye splice. The half-strands may be re-laid by using your fingers, but a better method is to take a small flat piece of wood and in it bore six holes in a circle with a seventh at the centre. Pass one half-strand through each hole and the half-heart through the centre one and, by twisting the wood round and round, re-lay the wire.

III. Joining Two Wire Ropes

To make a Short Splice. *1.* Put a firm, but narrow, whipping on both ropes about 18 in. from the end. *2.* Unlay to this point and cut out all hearts. *3.* Crutch the strands as for a Short Splice in hempen rope (except that there will be six to a side, not three). *4.* Put a firm seizing round the crutch to keep all parts in position whilst making the tucks.

5. Tuck each strand over the strand from the other rope to its immediate left and under the one beyond it, again as in hempen rope splicing. 6. Continue with two more full tucks and two 'thirded' ones on each rope, all left-handed, i.e. from right to left. 7. Cut and pick away the whippings. 8. Cut off all ends and serve.

A Short Splice cannot be used on a wire rope that has to pass through a block or pulley, as it is too bulky.

To make a Long Splice. As in hempen rope, a Long Splice should not increase the size of the wire and can therefore be used on a rope that has to pass through a block. However, it uses up a considerable amount of rope and it might be found more economical to obtain a new wire rather than to remove the weak portion of an old one with a Long Splice. In making wire rope slings (see Chapter 6) a Short Splice is usually employed, but if a continuous wire rope band without any bulges is needed, then a Long Splice must be used.

1. Unlay alternate strands of both ropes to a stout whipping for a distance which should be at least 12 ft. for a 1-in. rope, up to at least 30 ft. for a 3 in. and proportionate distances for intermediate sizes. This will leave three alternate strands on each rope unlaid and the other three still laid up round the heart. *2.* Cut these latter threes and the hearts about 6 in. from the whippings. Each rope now has three long and three short ends. *3.* Pull out the short lengths of heart and crutch the strands so that each long end is opposed to a short end of the other rope. *4.* Stop the long ends of rope 'A' to the standing part of rope 'B' to keep them out of the way temporarily. *5.* Cut off the whipping on rope 'A'. *6.* Further unlay one short end of rope 'A' and lay up the corresponding long end of rope 'B' in its place until only about 3 ft. of the long end remains. *7.* Lock the two ends by crossing them and cut off the rope 'A' end until it, too, is only about 3 ft. long. Similarly unlay the other two rope 'A' short ends and lay up the rope 'B' ends in their places and lock them. *9.* Cut the whipping on rope 'B' and lay the rope 'A' long ends up in place of the rope 'B' short ends and lock them.

The points of locking of opposing strands, i.e. the points up to which one strand is laid up in place of another, should be so arranged that they are equi-distant (Fig. 121). You

Fig. 121

may find that in the operation so far the assistance of at least one other person may be necessary, especially in crutching the strands tightly together, for if they are not so crutched an unsightly join will result.

Wire rope strands cannot be hitched, unfortunately, so the problem now arises of burying the ends in such a way that the strands will bind round them and hold them in position. This means that the hearts will have to be pulled out to make a space for the ends, but since the outside strands will not grip on the smooth surface of a buried wire, the ends must first be parcelled over with thin cloth or served with thin yarns. Further, they must each be cut to the exact length so that each, when buried, butts against the end of the one next to it. If two ends are too short so that they do not meet, the outer strands will sag into the empty space; if they are too long and overlap, the wire will bulge.

To bury the ends. *1.* Pull out the heart of rope 'A' to a point just past the first pair of locked ends. (Running a

spike along between the strands where the heart is emerging
will make it easier to pull the latter out.) *2*. Uncross the
lock. *3*. Insert the spike under the strand next to this first
loose end of rope 'A' and pass the point of the spike over
that end. *4*. Now, by moving the spike along the rope
towards the initial crutching point and at the same time
bearing down with its point on the loose end, the latter will
be found to disappear into the space left by the heart (Fig.
150*b*). *5*. Pull more of the heart out until it is over half-way
towards the next pair of locked ends. *6*. Using the spike as
in stages 3 and 4 but this time moving *away* from the crutch.
bury the loose end of rope 'B' previously locked with the
rope 'A' loose end already buried. *7*. Pull out more heart
and bury the next loose end of rope 'A', then that of rope
'B', then the third of rope 'A' and the third of rope 'B'.
8. Cut off the heart of rope 'A' and push the end into the
rope. *9*. Repeat stages 1 to 8 on rope 'B'. *10*. A little
hammering and twisting will put the rope back into shape
again, and the splice should be almost impossible to detect.
An alternative method is not to uncross the lock as in
stage 2, but to bury the ends using *two* spikes as shown in
the illustration (Fig. 122).

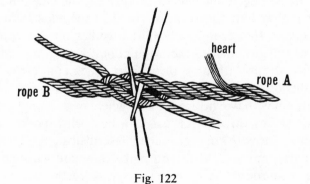

Fig. 122

To make a Wire Grommet. *1.* Extract a strand from a flexible steel wire rope equal in length to five and a half to six times the circumference of the desired grommet. If the finished ring is to be served, remember that this will reduce the inside circumference of the grommet and that the actual ring of wire will therefore need to be slightly larger. *2.* Towards one end of the strand, form a loop of the required size and half knot the ends, taking care to preserve the natural lay of the strand, i.e. if it is from a right-handed rope, then the right-hand end must be twisted over the left-hand, and *vice versa* if it is from a left-handed rope. *3.* Dog the longer end a number of times round the loop, keeping it in the natural curves of the lay, and then check that the loop is still the correct size. *4.* The long end must now be dogged round and round the loop to make five complete circuits (as in making a grommet with hempen rope, except that there only three complete circuits are made). After making the third circuit, it may be found that using a pricker or small spike will help to put the fourth properly into place, and the fifth circuit should be lightly hammered at every turn to lay the strand well in. *5.* Finish off this *five-part grommet* in one of the following ways: (a) if the grommet is to be parcelled and served, simply cut the ends off short so that they butt together; or (b) bury the ends as in long splicing so that they finally butt together on the opposite side of the grommet to the original half knot (this will give the five strands a heart); or (c) halve each end, cross them and dispose of them by tucking over one and under one.

You may have noticed that, whereas a hempen rope grommet has three parts just as a hempen rope has three strands, the wire rope grommet described above has only five parts, not six. When you make one, you will find that there is no room left for a sixth part. Nevertheless, the five-part grommet is widely and commonly used, although its strength should be taken as only about three-quarters of that of a flexible wire rope of the same diameter.

By taking more trouble, however, it is possible to make a *six-part grommet* with a single strand of wire. *1.* Carry out stages 1 to 4 as above but use a strand equal in length to about eight times the circumference of the desired grommet. *2.* After the fifth part has been laid in, take another strand of the same size equal in length to the grommet's circumference plus an inch or two and, with a pricker, work this into the centre of the five parts already laid up as a heart, leaving both ends sticking out. *3.* Now that the grommet has a heart, it will be found that there is room to lay in a sixth circuit with the original strand. Do this. *4.* Tuck both ends of the original strand through the grommet with three parts on either side of them. *5.* Pull out the temporary heart and lay up the ends in its place (as in Long Splicing). *6.* Cut them off so that they butt on the opposite side of the grommet.

Tailpiece

A Cautionary Anecdote. In 1940, as a new, young and very ordinary seaman, I was in a minelayer that caught fire with nearly six hundred mines aboard and had to be abandoned. At the order 'Abandon Ship!' a group of us tried to release a balsawood float. I cannot remember if it was held by slip shackles or not. If it was, then there could have been no hammer nearby with which to knock out their retaining pins, for I do remember that we tried to untie the knots of the lashings with our fingers. Sheathed as they were in paint and swollen with rain and sea water, all we achieved for our pains were broken fingernails.

And not one of us in that group had a knife! I knew where mine was: in my oilskin on the mess deck; but just then it might as well have been at the bottom of the Atlantic Ocean.

Well, we never did free that float and it went down with the ship—unlike the incompetent humans who were taken off in a motor-boat; but its undeserved end taught me a lesson that I now pass on. If you are ever where your life may depend upon ropes—afloat, on a mountain, up a tree or working on a roof—never be without a sharp knife, preferably one with a small marline-spike attached. Remember how Alexander the Great solved the most famous of all knotty problems: he slashed the Gordian Knot apart with his sword!

Index

149